Chapter

Cover credit to Leslie Tan, a loyal friend.

Foreword

This biography was written as a gift to Yoyo Yan.

If I have hit the target, this book will surprise you, it will provide a window for you to see some significant differences in eastern and western cultures, and hopefully it will inspire readers who may still have unfulfilled dreams.

The three main themes embedded into this biography are as follows:

➢ The long journey out of extreme poverty in rural China to become a respected journalist
➢ The struggle to accept and later embrace one's sexuality
➢ The relentless pursuit of becoming a parent

As I write this I am reflecting back on this project and the various chapters herein. Some chapters were so enjoyable to write. After you have read it, if you are so inclined I would love to hear from you. I am particularly interested in knowing which of the sections/chapters you enjoyed the most to see if they match up with mine. ☺

My personal email is: *mkevin1966@gmail.com*

June 2022. Newmarket, ON Canada

Chapter 1 *A Career Conundrum*

D awn broke with a spectacular sunrise on the fourth Monday of September in 2019, and that morning the long delay to receive "permanent residency" legal status ended with success. Zhonghua (Yoyo) Yan, the talented Chinese news agency reporter, was eager to find his first journalism job in Canadian media. That evening, he and Tony celebrated at their home with champagne and shrimp cocktail, and made a reservation for dinner at their favourite Toronto steakhouse. However, despite the long-awaited great news, a new challenge quickly emerged. Although Yoyo had a remarkable resume and was employable in both Chinese and English media, he found the labour market excruciatingly tight. He continued to network through Facebook and LinkedIn, and he diligently followed journalist postings on employment sites like Indeed. After over three months of frustration and disappointment, Yo was able to secure only one interview and no job offers. Growing increasingly impatient, he made up his mind that he must have something tangible to share with his family by Chinese New Year.

Husband Tony was busy working at the grocery store, so Yoyo had too much free time at his disposal. Yoyo filled his days by taking the always energetic Mac to his favourite dog parks and focusing on some of his own daily workout routines. At 176 cm tall and weighing only 63 kg, Yoyo was in good physical condition, stronger and leaner than ever before. Mulling over his options, he began to wonder: Could journalism be a dead end for a recent immigrant to Canada? Would Canadian employers allow him a level playing field, or would a resume identifying a degree from an unknown Chinese university and a name like Zhonghua keep him on the sidelines? Maybe it was time to switch his focus and pursue one of his other career dreams?

Many Canadian immigrants in his social network were telling him about the seemingly ubiquitous private sector employment barriers, and told tales of outright discrimination in some cases. With that nagging concern in mind, Yoyo decided he needed to revive his contingency plan - an idea he had mentioned to Tony several times during their marriage. He decided to go for it. He would now get serious about finding work in the public sector. Now was the time he would start the process of becoming a police officer.

The childhood dream of being a cop was still a vivid memory. As a smaller man, Yoyo always believed that law enforcement officers appeared larger, more handsome, and more powerful when in their uniforms. Admittedly, he wasn't excited about the dangers of patrolling the streets, but he figured with his skill set as a reporter he could ascend the ladder and become a detective at some point.

However, within days Yoyo found out that the qualifications and process for police training academy in Ontario are somewhat cumbersome and included mandatory volunteering experiences in Canada. He attended a videoconference session facilitated by the Toronto Police Services to learn more about the essential qualifications and their hiring process. But on a cold December day in 2019, just as he was starting down that road into law enforcement, gathering the necessary documentation and simultaneously fine-tuning his resume, Yoyo Yan's life took a sharp, sudden turn.

Kevin McCaffrey

Chapter 2 *Life on the Farm*

D aylight drifted to dusk, giving way to the night. Undeterred by the darkness, Yoyo and his sister Meiying created quite a commotion when they came inside to find their mother preparing the evening meal in their small kitchen. Unable to adjust the volume, two vibrant voices and youthful laughter brought the only form of electricity available into their small home in the rural village of Guoyuanchang, near the Jinjiang River, some 850 km west of Shanghai.

As mom prepared far less rice than she would have liked for the four of them, she continued to worry about her children - would they be silently feeling pangs of hunger when they are tucked into their shared bed? Similar thoughts no doubt crossed the minds of many parents in rural China, burdened with its surging population and a slowly evolving, command economy. Even the 1979 one child policy (that was strictly enforced for families living in bigger cities) and other social reforms did not resolve the food insecurity faced by Yoyo and his family in 1989. On that night, his mom's fears would indeed become a reality, and two tiny stomachs did gently rumble as they slept.

A lack of manufactured toys certainly did not deter the two youngsters from finding ways to entertain themselves. And the absence of furniture is a blessing when you are a kid, it leaves more room for creative play. Ten year old Meiying, adored her younger brother and encouraged him to use his imagination as they found things to do together.

Although they had never been to the symphony, they had never owned a record, and their battered radio transmitted mostly news, Yoyo and Meiying created a joyful song together. They alternated between singing and humming in Mandarin:

Take me to the river

Show me the rocks covered in moss

Ohhh, what a beautiful sight

Take me to river

Show me a pathway to cross

Ohhh, what a beautiful sight

*Just remember to **hold on tight***

After cleaning the dishes, mom and dad joined the children in the other room. Only a few candles illuminated the living area as they came together for some family time; the only time they gathered together all day. Most days Dad got out of bed at sunrise and left for work before the cargo arrived at the local railway station, before little Yoyo awakened. Thus, the evenings were the epicenter of their laughter, life lessons and sharing of folklore.

Chinese culture focuses on duty to family, tradition, and pride like few cultures do. In a society where expectations are high, where conformity trumps individuality, and where social contracts related to family are so ingrained, Yoyo and Meiying soaked up their parent's lessons and values like sponges. In China, pathways to perceived success prescribe a traditional family unit with parents in full control of decision making, in a nod to the Communist Party's legacy. It would take many years before Yoyo would begin to question some of the most rigid family expectations;

especially the one about finding a good wife as soon as possible.

Yoyo and his sister remained largely oblivious to their circumstances, and they knew nothing about the bright lights and relative prosperity that are found in Shanghai and Beijing. They walked almost 60 minutes to get to their school, an aging building where many desirable resources for teachers and students were missing. Aging blackboards and a few posters lined the walls of the primary school, but the aging desks were carved and marked up by former students. While in the third grade, Yoyo and the other students learned some of their math skills sharing one abacus and they all knew they must keep a close eye on the one pencil they will be given for the school year. Regardless of the dearth of academic resources, Yoyo loved his time in school. He made friends easily and always looked forward to his boxed lunch, which was occasionally filled with tasty chestnuts. Yoyo did not realize it at age 8, but his natural curiosity and ability to retain information easily would certainly take him to some interesting places.

Meiying was and still is Yoyo's best friend and confidant. Meiying was born 20 months prior but in the early grades the two siblings were always in the same small classes. Their parents had arranged for that goal willfully, by delaying their daughter's enrollment into school until she was age 6. Instinctively, the parents knew that their children may face hardships and fatigue on the long walk to school, and occasional bullying from aggressive kids from the bigger villages. Before the rather shy Yoyo found his self-confidence and grew wings, Meiying was his advisor and loyal protector. Their strong bond continues to this day, despite living on different sides of the world.

Children learn more by observation than by other means. Yoyo admired his older sister and has always watched her with a keen eye. His unyielding sense of optimism emanates from Yoyo's relationship with his elder sister. As a teenager, one of the many things he learned by watching Meiying is that one needs to be determined regardless of one's current circumstances. Meiying yearned to become a success in business despite the often overt discrimination against girls that existed in Chinese culture. Meiying was always a goal-oriented girl. She studied hard, and today she is successfully juggling her career in accounting while raising her two adorable children near the heart of Beijing.

One of Yoyo's friends, Qiuling, was one of twin boys who lived in the same village. Qiuling's father found work in Shanggao, manufacturing sewing machines. That income allowed for a slightly more privileged life than most living in Guoyuanchang. Qiuling showed up on the narrow road outside their home one day sitting high atop his lime green bicycle – with the blessing of a small taste of freedom granted his doting, habitually cautious parents.

"Yoyo, I'm out in the street," he exclaimed. "Come see what my father got for me."

Young Yoyo had seen cartoonish images of a bicycle in a couple of the books he borrowed from school, but he had never actually seen a real one up close. He dashed out of the family home to find his friend with a gleeful expression, as Qiuling awkwardly dismounted his bicycle and stumbled as it fell onto the dirt laneway. Yoyo became so excited he could barely get words to flow, but when he did he blurted out:

"You....you ride that from house? Can I try? Please!"

His buddy hesitated for a moment, surprised that his smaller friend would be that courageous, with the realization that riding it is not as easy as it seems in fantasy. Upon seeing

Yoyo's excitement, Qiuling relented and with a steadying hand he hoisted the right half of Yoyo over the middle bar and up onto the hard iron seat.

"Hold on tight," Qiuling warned.

Yoyo could barely contain his zeal. He tried to pedal and go forward, but his first ride did not go well. Almost immediately after Qiuling let go of the handlebars, Yoyo found himself unbalanced and in a sense of panic like he had never felt before. Predictably, he took a hard tumble within seconds. His right leg burned from the impact and his elbow began to throb with pain. Fortunately, no real damage was done to Qiuling's prized possession. A good cold water cleansing and the last dollop squeezed from the neighbour's tube of antibiotic lotion was mother's remedy, but a sleepless night ensued for Yoyo. Despite his dreadful cycling debut, for several months Yoyo thought about that bicycle, and how lucky his friend was to have one. He never mentioned his yearning for a bicycle to his parents, but did bring it up to Meiying on more than one occasion.

Becoming a fighting soldier never really appealed to Yoyo as a boy, but men in uniform always seemed to capture his attention. Police and military officers, in particular, fascinated young Yoyo. In the same way that superheroes like Batman and Superman appeal to so many young North American boys, Yoyo was fascinated by the power and control raciating from the uniformed officers of the state. One day right before a school holiday period in 1991, Yoyo had a rare encounter with a firefighter who came to the school to provide fire safety tips for students. He arrived wearing a bright orange kit, which included a zip up jacket and loose fitting, comfortable pants with yellow reflective striping across his chest and on forearms and above his ankles. A white domed helmet sat atop his head and black, shiny, lace-up boots completed his uniform.

Shortly after the uniformed firefighter arrived in the classroom, fear and terror overcame Yoyo. Suddenly, various scenes of flames and screaming paralyzed Yoyo as he sat at his desk. As the firefighter began to speak, Yoyo processed not a word - he just started sobbing uncontrollably. After he put his head on his desk, his teacher and the guest stopped talking. Quickly, they walked over to Yo's desk at the back of the room.

"Yoyo, what on earth is the matter? Yoyo?" asked Mr. Li. "Our guest is a good man, he only comes to help us understand the dangers of fire."

After a couple of minutes of unresponsive sobbing, the puzzled and concerned teacher asked the stronger guest to pick little Yoyo up and carry him to the staff lounge, where he could be isolated from his classmates. The friendly firefighter returned to the classroom and finished his presentation and took the students' questions, minus one distraught student.

The schoolmaster came to the staff room to console Yoyo, and eventually Yoyo was able to whisper some of his thoughts and fears in staccato language: "fire...sister. Mom! MOM...help!" Only an hour later, when Yoyo's mother was summoned to the school to pick him up and take him home early, were the school officials able to learn about the source of this indelible trauma. Mother gave them the short version of the fire in the family home when Yoyo was a toddler. A brief blaze had started one afternoon when the children were playing near a charcoal fireplace - they had knocked it onto the ground from its perch on the table. As flames began to spread, it took young Yoyo a few seconds to assess the danger before he made it into an adjacent room, and eventually outside. As a result, her only son endured both emotional and physical scarring.

Hold on Tight

Physically, Yoyo had second degree burns on the back of his head, and more serious third degree burns on a significant area of skin on the left upper leg and left buttocks. As an adult, Yoyo would eventually accept this permanent scarring with the help of a well-designed tattoo. Emotionally, the fire and its aftermath seemed to strengthen his resolve to be successful, and to help his family improve their circumstances.

Chapter 3 *Mr. Tutu*

L ooking back, Yoyo and so many other Chinese born in the 1980s benefitted from the reforms and the long awaited opening-up policy of Deng Xiaoping. Those reforms seemed to be implemented with the goal of increasing social mobility for those individuals who would dream big, seizing some new opportunities. The reconfigured curricula had a new focus on practical and experiential learning embedded with threads of a newer, less repressive kind of socialist ideology. That was slowly shifting from the long lectures based on Confucius principles which had stifled critical thinking and risk taking. Some students at Shanggao No.2 High School found that change intoxicating, and Yoyo was one of them.

On Deng's directive, higher education became far more accessible to those in poverty, and universities and colleges became more socio-economically integrated. Although it was mostly in Yoyo's unconscious mind, those reforms and the more egalitarian approach to public education enabled Yoyo to dream, to be optimistic about his future. His family's lack of wealth and social status were disadvantageous; nonetheless, a young mind goes to places it needs to go.

High school would bring personal growth, new challenges, a new best friend, and most importantly an influential mentor for Yoyo, Mr. Tutu. He had big dreams in his pre-teen and teenage years. Somewhat instinctively, he seemed to be drawn to live in a bigger city and to become bilingual, amongst other desires. He presciently believed that learning another language would open up the world for him, as he thought about leaving the simple country life behind. Yo started to enjoy his lessons in language arts, particularly when learning some basic English. By the age of 14, Yoyo could name most of the colours and animals in English. He was especially fond of talking and learning about bears, and learning about their lives and habitats. He began to use his animal words in English whenever he had the opportunity, causing his classmates to giggle in bewilderment. Eventually, one of his mates nicknamed Yoyo as Nóngmín 農民, which translates to the farmer. Much later in life, Yoyo would turn a yearning for owning animals into a reality when he adopted his first dog, Macchiato.

Hui Xiong was Yoyo's best friend during this period of his evolving life. Hui, a much larger boy with his black hair in a crew cut, was affectionately known as "Bear" to his close friends. Bear was an only child, who eventually graduated at the top of the class and had the unique opportunity to attend Massachusetts Institute of Technology (MIT) to study theoretical physics. But at that point during the boys' second year of senior secondary school their desire to attend university required personal discipline - and many hours of studying after the formal school day concluded. Bear had recently reached age 16, and like most boys his age he was easily distracted. Much to his parents' dismay, Bear spent countless hours entertaining himself with games of table tennis, crime novels, and comic books when he should have been doing his homework. Fortunately, Yoyo's steady temperament and sense of duty served as a guiding light for him, and Bear gradually matured out of his adolescent exploits. His self-control, his motivation, in fact his entire future rose like a phoenix after meeting and befriending Yoyo.

Sadly, Yoyo and his father became distant during his high school years, barely talking during 1997. The genesis of their conflict is complex and not entirely clear, but it could have been that father's expectations were too suffocating and he needed to create space to grow into a more independent young man. As a teenager, Yoyo was quietly yearning for a kind, intellectual mentor.

Fortunately, during high school, Mr. Zhengjian Tutu arrived in his life. Tutu was a young, energetic teacher. Although he followed the social norm and married a woman at age 28, he was also more than a little bit of a non-conformist in conservative China. He was tall and fit from his daily exercise and jogging routines. Tutu had no trouble getting the students' attention, as he spoke thoughtfully but with a distinct, deep baritone voice Yoyo had never heard before. Although Mr. Tutu was a very influential teacher to all, he seemed to spend more time with Yoyo and Bear than many of the other kids. Yo was drawn to his teacher, shifting between exhilaration, confusion, and admiration at various times.

One sunny day in the fall season, Tutu's class headed out on a field trip to a local garden, for a botany related science lesson. As they approached the garden, the uneven, difficult roadway descended gradually adjacent to a weed covered fieldstone wall. At Yoyo's height, he tried unsuccessfully to climb over the wall from the roadway up onto the terrain above. Instinctively, the taller, stronger teacher extended his right hand to help. Yoyo grabbed Mr. Tutu's hand and pulled himself up to join his teacher and the other boys on the terrain above. Yoyo, momentarily speechless, felt his heartbeat quicken. It was a feeling he had so rarely experienced in his 16 years....the strength and warmth of an older man's touch.

This period of his life was so confusing. Is it possible to be attracted to your teacher at the tender age of 16? What kind of attraction is this? Maybe it is simply admiration, a desire to grow up and be just like him? Why does my heart skip a beat when my teacher leans over my desk to point something out in my work? Why does an image of my teacher so often pop into my head when I am settling into bed?' So many questions, and no clear answers, yet.

One thing Yoyo knew for sure was that he could not disclose his attraction to and affection for his teacher to *anyone.* Boys and young men in China, and most other places around the world, were loath to discuss any same sex attractions, lest they be caught up in the tangled web of bullying, name calling and potential isolation. The vocal majority perceived being gay as a perversion, as a mental illness. Consequently, Yoyo became distracted by other endeavours and tried valiantly to suppress and forget about his feelings for Mr. Tutu after the science trip. Coincidently, 1997 was actually the same year that consensual same sex activity was finally legalized in the People's Republic; and four years later LGBTQ people no longer had to deal with the stigma of being believed to be mentally ill. The needle was moving towards acceptance; albeit very slowly.

Meanwhile, in Physical Education class later that year Yoyo had a memorable moment in the boys' change room. One day as a few students were in the midst of putting on their ill-fitting athletic shorts, Yoyo saw something very mysterious, something very memorable - the erection of a classmate. Michael's royal blue brief style underwear had a slotted opening that provided Yoyo with a brief look. Yoyo saw the front half of it, noting its rigidity and its beauty. Yoyo did not want to be caught staring at his friend so he quickly averted his glance elsewhere...but that brief alluring image endured.

With his academics Yoyo was always very focused on his class ranking. He was dreaming again, and this time his dream focused on attending Tsinghua University in Beijing.

Most years, less than 1% of the senior students who write the ubiquitous *Gaokao* test are admitted to prestigious universities like Peking and Tsinghua. Because of China's rather controversial quota system of regional acceptances, it is actually much easier for students in urban areas to get into the most desired universities than it is for people living in rural towns like Guoyuanchang. Sometimes, a post-secondary institution takes so few students from a rural province that it does not offer many of its programs to them, significantly limiting the graduating student's options.

Yoyo studied hard and rarely engaged in recreation. His "bookworm" reputation was well-earned; Yoyo was rewarded by gaining the #1 ranking in his class of 40. He wrote the notoriously difficult eight hour Chinese university entrance exam in July of 1998 and then anxiously awaited the result to see if he would be able to punch his ticket to Beijing. Six weeks later, Yo received word that he had failed to score high enough on the exam in order to achieve his goal. Young Yoyo was crushed, and didn't eat for days. Yoyo was reeling, and needed time to accept his fate.

After some guidance from Mr. Tutu and others, Yoyo and a couple of his other classmates decided that they would enroll in a second tier university far from the bright lights of Beijing. After graduation, he prepared himself for a 22 hour train ride southwest. He planned to spend the next four years of his life in Chengdu, a city known for its hot weather and hotspots for gay scenes, but Yoyo wouldn't know the latter until years after he left the city.

Chapter 4 *Leaps of Faith*

I n September of 1998 Yoyo began his first year of post-secondary studies at Chengdu University. He wandered around the campus in that first week, mesmerized by the dazzling Russian architecture and the gleaming new buildings. The library in particular was a thing of beauty, with alternating horizontal bands of opaque rose and transparent glass encompassing its entire girth. It was by far the biggest and most impressive building Yoyo had ever seen. Yoyo stopped to admire it from afar, then approached the front entry doors. Yoyo felt so many emotions within his first few days away from home, but fear was not one of them. He was excited to meet his new teachers and new classmates.

Chengdu University was rarely a destination of choice for very high achievers like Yoyo. Built in 1956, it was a fairly new institution. Chengdu was filled with younger, inexperienced faculty and fewer students studying math, technology and sciences. Other programs at Chengdu were related to the humanities, cultures of the world, and languages. Although he did not realize it the previous year during acceptance season, failing to meet the highest standard on the rigorous entrance exams helped to shape Yoyo's future. While many students at Chengdu stood compliantly on this ower rung of the social ladder, Yoyo was an outlier. He was motivated to climb higher for a better view.

During the autumn and winter of his first year at Chengdu, he would spend his days with the obligatory 9-10 hours in classrooms with his peers. Yoyo, however, sought more in his hunger for learning. On a typical day, Yoyo would take a dinner break for an hour or less, and force himself into study sessions which, more times than not, ended after midnight. During that first year, Yoyo took courses which included literature, physical education, physics, and math. It was at this point in his journey that he truly realized his love of the English language and all its beauty and complexities. In addition, he believed that being bilingual could be his ticket to unknown, alluring destinations outside China. In a few years, he would be proven correct.

Although idle time was scarce, athletics and recreation became more important to Yoyo during his university years. When he could find a racquet to borrow, he played some badminton with his classmates. He also began to enjoy swimming; although not without an embarrassing moment. His freshman year allowed for one physical education choice, and Yoyo chose Learn to Swim. There were no swimming pools back home in Guoyuanchang so he was a bit naive about certain 'necessities' one needs to participate in public swimming. He was about to discover one of them on the first day of Learn to Swim class. Moments after he emerged on the pool deck for the first time, an instructor approached him hastily and began scolding him. Young Yoyo was standing there in his underwear, unaware that wearing a proper swimsuit was required.

Of the 34 students in his English class - Yoyo always achieved at the #1 or #2 ranking. His work was often outstanding, and his normally stoic professors fueled his inner fire by offering occasional praise. He composed a particularly introspective, raw poem about courage in 1999.

Hold on Tight

A Warm Embrace

Another lonely day not feeling entirely whole
I finally met a man who looked into my soul

The key to my heart is so elusive
The ones I yearn for are not so effusive
Opportunities come, opportunities go
Was he the one - how was I to know?
Do I silently struggle on, or should I risk a disgrace
With a leap of faith and a warm embrace

Courageous Rosa chose her seat on that bus
Knowing quite well it would kick up a fuss
Our past is now lost, so a price has been paid
For those of us in turmoil, now finally swayed
Should I continue to lie, or should I go to his place
With a leap of faith and a warm embrace

A Warm Embrace was only the third poem Yo had written as an undergraduate English student, but he was totally immersed in it. He spent hours deliberating over the prose, the confusing angst he felt, and the overall structure to make it flow better. Fortunately, he sensed that Professor Dee wanted her students to write from their hearts, and speak their truths. Consequently, at 18 years of age Yoyo found his voice.....he found the courage to submit this poem, and for the first time tacitly admitted his occasional attraction to men. He felt an odd mix of fear and liberation.

Alas, in his first few months at Chengdu, Yoyo did not find his warm embrace. His fear was that any leap of faith might end up like Icarus' doomed encounter with the sun. However, shortly before the New Year celebrations began, fear finally yielded to courage. One Sunday shortly after he started playing, Yoyo found himself in a game of badminton doubles. One of Yoyo's classmates was on the other side of the net, playing with his friend Samson. Samson was about the same height as his opponents, but had a different physique. At the top of his ripped trapezius muscles, his shoulders were wide, which allowed his back to fill out his t-shirt quite nicely. Yoyo noticed that his torso was slightly shorter than most; which made his shapely legs seem long for his height. His hair was cut short in the back, but wispy and longer in the front. As Samson moved quickly around the court his bangs flirted with his forehead like silk tassels moving in a gentle breeze. Yoyo's heart rate escalated.

Yoyo and his partner were clearly at a competitive disadvantage in this contest. Although they did win a few points here and there, their opponents were very skilled shot makers and Samson, in particular, was able to cover the court like a gazelle. Of course it didn't help that Yoyo was often admiring his opponent's physical attributes while he should have been adjusting his position to defend his side. At one point, a hopeful yet entirely unhelpful thought popped into his head. I hope he has to turn around and run for a bird so I can get a good look at his bum....he thought just as another shot landed adjacent to him - another lost point.

After about 40 minutes the game concluded with quick handshakes at the net. Although all four of them had plans to study later in the day, they sat briefly in the common area before departing for the recreation center. Yoyo overheard his classmate ask Samson when he was scheduled to work next. Instantly Yo put that into memory. He was curious to know where exactly Samson worked, learning about this gorgeous guy's life. He would later find out that Samson was a year older and in a different program, studying accounting. The job they were referring to was a part-time job in the Ito Yokado mall selling athletic apparel.

One week later, with some help from friends on campus, Yoyo was able to deduce that Samson was likely working at a store called *Life Infiniti Outdoor Sports Shop*. Long before he knew what the word "stalking" meant, Yoyo began to think about what reason he could create to pay a visit to that store to catch another glimpse of this mysterious man. The pretense of shopping for new athletic shorts and maybe some new shoes seemed like it would suffice.

On the following Saturday afternoon, after a study session, Yo decided he would take a leap of faith and try to find Samson. Evidently it did not occur to him that even if he was able to time his arrival at the store when his target was actually working, it was entirely possible Samson would not recognize him. Additionally, it was also unlikely there would be much time for chit chat while a man was working the sales floor in a very public space. Instead, Yoyo wrestled with his inner voice.... do I have the nerve to take that leap of faith, to seek that warm embrace? Despite all of the potential risks, Yoyo got off the bus and made his way inside the mall about an hour before it closed for the day.

He arrived at *Life Infiniti* thinking that he would try to act like a random customer with money to spend. Unfortunately, as he crossed the threshold into the store, a wave of anxiety momentarily shook his confidence. How could he simultaneously shop and flirt without it being too obvious that flirting was his primary motive? Was this a terrible idea? Did Samson have a girlfriend? Maybe he already had a more attractive boyfriend? Was Samson so straight he would ignore whatever flirtatious comments came his way? Worse, would he be offended and abruptly out Yoyo to some of their mutual friends back on campus? Most LGBTQ people have had social situations when they had to endure such thoughts and the anxiety that accompanies them. Usually, dating experience and a very confident approach is the remedy for those apprehensions. Yoyo brought neither to the mall that day.

After locating *Life Infiniti*, Yoyo peered around the store to see if he could locate the object of his desires. As soon as his eyes came upon handsome Samson, his heart skipped a beat and he quickly looked down at a display of shirts to his right. He gathered himself briefly, as he tested the garment's fabric with a touch. Shortly after that false start, he noticed Samson was not engaged with any customers or staff, since his associate had moseyed into the back room to find a product for one of the few customers currently in the store. This appeared to be his opportunity for the highly anticipated approach.

"Hey! I think I know you," said Yoyo with as much confidence as he could muster.

"Uh, hmmmm. Yes, yes I think you are studying at Chengdu, right? We met somewhere on campus?" came the reply from Samson, with what sounded like a slight tone of enthusiasm.

"Yes we did. We played badminton together in the rec center. You were partnered with Miao."

"You're a very good badminton player," Yoyo continued, with increasing confidence.

Samson countered with a slight laugh and a stunning smile that lit up Yoyo's eyes.

"Not really, but I do play often."

Sensing an opening….Yoyo said:

"Oh that's nice. We should play again sometime soon."

If *Life Infiniti* had sold racquets Yoyo would have stripped down to his shorts and t-shirt and suggested a game right there in the mall to maximize their time together. Instead he paused and waited, hoping to get a positive reply to his offer. Instead, Samson ignored the suggestion and moved the conversation in a different direction.

"Are you looking for anything in particular here today?"

Yoyo paused, startled by the question and its various connotations.

"Ummm, yes I am." After a brief pause he continued without risking the awkward truth that the particular thing was a person. "I am thinking about buying some new shorts for my badminton games."

"Oh, ok then I can take you over to our men's shorts displays. Sorry I don't remember your name…"

"Yoyo….. I am Yoyo Yan."

As the two men moved towards the display Samson asked,

"Yoyo, that's a unique name, what is the significance of it? Is it a traditional family name?"

"No not really, just my name I guess. So how long have you been working here?"…which seemed like a better question in his mind than it actually sounded as it lingered awkwardly in the air between them.

"Not that long," Samson replied somewhat dismissively.

After a few more innocuous comments mostly related to brands and his purchase options….the conversation took one more turn, and Yoyo sensed a feeling of **now or never.**

"So I just remembered your name, it's Samson right? But I don't really know how to find you at the university if you want to meet up sometime," Yoyo said. The short silence that followed as Samson processed the comment seemed like five minutes, though it was less than five seconds.

"Yes, I am Samson. Your memory is good. Well, why don't you give me your residence name and room number - I will call you for a game sometime."

Though his mind was cluttered with some of the prose from *The Warm Embrace*, his smile came easily as he gathered himself and gave Samson his contact information. Trying to be casual, Yoyo spent another 10 minutes feigning interest in some of the products on display, but eventually left the store without making a purchase.

Although it took almost an hour and one bus transfer for Yoyo to return to campus, he had little recollection of the journey. He was deep in thought, imagining how a date with Samson would look, feel, maybe even taste if he could steal a kiss. When he arrived home to an empty residence, the waiting game began. After about two full days without hearing from Samson, he was dealing with a nagging thought that maybe he had made a mistake. Perhaps it was caused by an inexperienced flirting maneuver; a decision which can cause an uneasy feeling of helplessness. He had not requested Samson's contact information; thus, he had given up full control of the outcome.

Three weeks later, on a damp and dreary Sunday morning just after Chinese New Year celebrations ended, the phone rang. The answering machine took calls after the 5th ring, so Yoyo scrambled out of the shower in time to pick up the call. Suddenly, the day brightened considerably.

"Hello, good morning" was his greeting.

"Hi Yoyo, Samson calling."

"Yes....ummmm, hi there, ahhhh how are you doing?"

"I am good, thanks. So I had a badminton game scheduled for today with Miao, but he isn't yet back to campus. When he called me to send his regrets a few minutes ago, I thought of our conversation in the store. What are your plans for early afternoon?"

"Oh man I thought you were never going to...... ummm no I mean I was really hoping.........no, ummmm, no I don't have plans....except maybe do some push-ups and pull-ups here in my room."

"I see. Well if you're free at 2 o'clock we can play for an hour under my reservation."

"Yes, Samson. Yes, definitely free. I will meet you out front of the rec center 10 minutes before, ok?"

"Cool that works. See you over there."

"Ok, ok bye." Yoyo stammered as he moved the phone away from his ear with his mind racing.

Eventually he put the phone back into its cradle and sat down. Yoyo came up with a plan, and that plan had nothing to do with winning badminton games. By the time he walked over to the rec center he had decided that right after the match ended he would offer to buy them both an energy drink in the lounge adjacent to the courts. Then, if they sat together privately, he would steer the conversation in a direction where he could ask about Samson's girlfriend to simultaneously open the window to his sexuality, and to try to discern how available Samson might be. This truly was becoming a leap of faith. His giant leap was airborne, but could he stick the landing?

The badminton games went as expected with Samson barely breaking a sweat. But they were simply a means to an end. The post-game chat, however, did not go as expected. Samson slipped in a reference about his girlfriend shortly after they began talking. The excitement of being with Samson dissipated quickly, and after some idle chat about his girlfriend and their respective courses and professors, they left the rec center and went on about their lives.

During his time in Chengdu University, Yoyo's self-confidence blossomed in ways unrelated to romance. He kept in close contact with his family, but visited them back home less and less often. Instead, as he made more friends, he spent more time on campus completing his English course assignments and immersing himself in campus life. Yoyo's focus and priorities shifted somewhat during this phase of his life. As a boy he was always a giver, sensitive to others' needs often at the expense of his own. But at Chengdu, he no longer felt it was his duty to help others. Instead, he focused more time working on his own goals and dreams, often insulating himself to the requests of his most demanding friends. He was no longer afraid to say no, and became more focused on finding a life passion.

He was determined to be successful, and build a wealth that would allow him to provide for his parents by the time they became elderly. Although Yoyo put up some boundaries during this time in order to focus only on his academics – that changed when he met Aki.

Aki Zhang, had just turned 20 when he arrived in Yoyo's life. He was taller and quite a bit heavier than Yoyo, but Aki was trying to get fit with his daily swimming and racquet sports. He had started at Chengdu after a gap year, so he was in the same class as Yoyo, studying English. Yoyo noticed him straight away, thinking that Aki was both attractive and friendly. Due to deeply engrained fears as a result of Chinese traditions, beliefs, and laws regarding homosexuality, neither of them had ever kissed - much less dated - a person of the same gender before. The next several months were a very discreet, yet exciting time for Yoyo. He and Aki were living together, sharing the same dormitory room together with six other guys.

One day after a lengthy, solitary study session analyzing the evolution of European literature, Yoyo found a book titled _Sexuality in China, Histories of Power & Pleasure_ in the University library. He decided to borrow it, although he had no idea when he could find the time to read it given all of the other assignments he was dealing with. Over the next six weeks, Yoyo was only able to get through about half of the book, but he found what he read fascinating and enlightening. He made a decision to read as much of it as he could prior to the summer recess, and finish reading it in the fall, if necessary. Taking it home with him for the summer was just too risky, in case his mother or father happened to find it and began asking probing questions he was not at all ready to answer.

Sexuality in China opened his eyes to many facets of Chinese history including the existence of all sorts of consensual relationships. In ancient times, polyamorous, homosexual, and especially extra-marital affairs were quite common. He learned that several Chinese emperors are thought to have had both heterosexual and same sex relationships. Brothels were found all over the vast country.

In certain regions especially in the north and west, men would sometimes even allow travelers to sleep with their wives during their stopovers! However, for most of the 1900s, homosexuality was kept in the shadows of Chinese society. As he read on, Yoyo realized how fortunate he was for the liberating 1997 legalization act, just as he became an adult. Obviously, old beliefs and stigmas are not replaced by new ones rapidly. Homosexual acts (or the *passion of Longyang* as some Chinese historians reference gay sex), are still widely perceived as a mental illness by older generations. Moreover, in modern day China, the Communist Party and state controlled media does not demonize LGBTQ citizens; but instead simply chooses to ignore them. Of course, like most controversial issues, gay rights are more openly discussed and accepted on university campuses throughout the mainland; even more so in Hong Kong and Taiwan.

Despite the obvious fear of being outed, Yoyo's world in Chengdu was changing quickly as he stumbled into his first tender relationship with a man. Approaching age 20 and with such limited experience with either gender, Yoyo had no idea how best to subtly communicate his attraction to Aki. It was an internal struggle that arrived into his conscious mind more often that he would have liked. It was becoming a distraction to him, and Yoyo often wondered if, and probably unconsciously wished, it was a passing phase. For almost six months, the two friends talked, studied, ate food and played tennis together; sans physical contact.

One of the things Yoyo loved about their friendship was how kind Aki was to him. Aki's kindness and reciprocal attraction first became apparent to Yoyo during the evenings in the spring of 2000. His best friend was the one who provided him with his own umbrella during rainstorms, smuggled food into the library to provide Yoyo with late night snacks during study time, and tried to make him laugh when Aki believed Yo was taking himself too seriously. Aki's joie de vivre and playfulness surfaced on many occasions.

One Saturday night, well after darkness had settled in, Yoyo arrived home from a lengthy study session to find more than 100 large, fully inflated balloons of various colours filling his room. They were so crammed into the space, that when he opened the door to enter, a couple of them broke free from containment and drifted out into the hallway. The others remained inside, and required Yoyo to barge through them with arms flailing to move around.

On another occasion Aki's prank was much simpler to pull off. That day, the boys were writing together in Aki's much larger apartment, preparing their creative writing assignments that were due the next day. In his living space there were two toilets, the bigger one was located in an ensuite bathroom attached to the master bedroom, and there was a small powder room for guests to use right next to the small kitchen. Knowing they would need to work all evening, and well past midnight, Aki anticipated that Yoyo would need a bathroom break or two. He pranked Yoyo by replacing the guest bathroom toilet paper roll with a large roll of gray duct tape. He had moved the toilet paper from the powder room and hid it under the kitchen sink earlier in the day. He was looking forward to hearing the cry for help from his friend after Yoyo had done his business and realized his predicament.

It was during some of those acts of kindness, compassion, and general silliness that Yoyo began to fall in love for the first time. He sensed he might actually love Aki after realizing that some of the warning signs had suddenly entered his daily life. For one, he would not make plans with other friends very often, trying to keep himself available for late night and weekend fun with Aki...just in case he called. Somewhat alarmingly, Yoyo also started to lose focus on his English professor during classes they attended together. He was daydreaming about Aki. The other indicator was how sad he felt on the rare weekends when they weren't able to see one another. When you have one eye on your work and the other on the wall phone hoping it rings, it's likely that you are falling in love.

Finally, after almost 10 months of friendship, the latent attraction was allowed to surface. One Friday during one of their schoolwork sessions at Aki's place they decided to take a break. Aki had been laying on the floor awkwardly and mentioned that his back hurt. Instinctively and without any hesitation, Yoyo told him to sit up and he would massage his back for him. Aki seemed surprised but followed his friend's command. Yoyo quickly repositioned himself on the couch, seated upright with his legs spread far enough apart for a human to wedge between them.

"Let me know where it hurts," Yoyo said in a soft voice.

"Ok. Well it's all the way down the left side, lower half" was Aki's reply.

After 15 seconds of gentle rubbing, Yoyo hit the spot.

"Right there, yes, ohhhh ohhhh yes, that's the spot."

Not much more was said as Yoyo experimented with his first ever back massage for the next few minutes. Eventually, Aki asked if Yoyo wanted him to return the favour, alluding to a switching of positions.

"Sure Aki, but let me continue helping you a bit longer."

"Ok, just let me know when you're ready."

"I will honey," Yoyo said, using his first term of endearment for Aki.

The term 'honey' startled Aki, but he didn't say anything….he sat and took his massage in silence. The mutual massaging ended after about 15 minutes, and they decided it would be a good time to make some food, since it was the dinner hour. Off to the kitchen they went, after having just crossed the threshold of physical contact, with the first hint of physical intimacy in their long friendship.

After they ate some rice and vegetables, they cleaned up the kitchen area together. Aki mentioned that his back felt better, and thanked Yo for his efforts. Suddenly, Aki put down the bowls, and used both hands to grab Yoyo by the hips - he swiveled him so the friends were now face to face. Somewhat aggressively, Aki pressed his full lips up against Yoyo's narrower lips. His aggression startled his smaller friend and Yoyo took a stumbling step backwards, feeling his back pressed up against the kitchen wall. A large skillet fell to the floor with a loud clang. Aki did not relent - he continued to forcefully kiss Yoyo. Inexperienced Yoyo was not sure if this was what kissing somebody always felt like, but it certainly was different from the kisses he held in his fantasies. His virgin lips ached for the next few minutes.

Yoyo and Aki remained very close friends and had intermittent romantic encounters as they moved towards completion of their undergraduate studies. They remained very discreet, since neither of them was comfortable with their same sex attraction. Those years were possibly best described as the Q in LGBTQ - a "questioning" phase of life. When they were not studying together, they enjoyed occasional playful banter and forbidden visits as the two slept in their bunk beds; but mostly they were just close friends sharing their goals and big dreams with one another.

Chapter 5 *Beijing or Bust*

While those university years provided Yoyo with much knowledge, personal growth, self-confidence, and his first love, graduation from Chengdu University was looming. Yoyo was fully aware that he soon needed to make a big decision about his future. He knew he wanted to begin a new chapter, but where and how?

Yoyo's work was widely respected by his peers, and his grades reflected his talents in languages and literature. Shortly after the final term began, in February 2002, his university offered him a placement for a concurrent Masters plus Doctoral program of study; a combined degree in Linguistics. It included a scholarship and bursaries that would cover his tuition costs, and would also provide him a modest amount to spend on his needs. For many, this offer would have been an easy lay-up. But Yo decided that he had bigger dreams. The appeal of living in new places he recalled reading and hearing about as a boy was overwhelming. He still desperately wanted to study in Beijing, to make his family, and especially Mr. Tutu, proud of him. He decided not to accept Chengdu's offer to stay.

For the second time in his young life, he would apply to a prestigious learning institution in Beijing; but this time he had his sights set on Peking University's Master's degree. He was feeling very confident based upon his academic standing as an undergraduate, so, in late March, he gathered the many required documents and posted them.

Hold on Tight

His application led to an in-person interview request from the admissions office at Peking U. If one is familiar with the vastness of China's topography, you realize that getting to the country's capital city is no easy task from Sichuan province. However, Yoyo was determined to interview, so he booked his ticket on the high speed, overnight train, known locally as the T8.

The exhilaration of going to Beijing for the first time began to take hold a week before he departed, and escalated daily. He yearned to contact Mr. Tutu to share his excitement, but decided against it until after he returned with the acceptance offer. Finally, on a Sunday evening in April 2002, Yoyo packed a small suitcase with his most formal attire and called a taxi. He was headed for the North station.

After boarding the T8 that would take him 2,121 km northeast, Yoyo tried to sleep. Instead he decided he would spend some time reading just to keep busy until he could fall asleep. While he was securing his belongings above his seat upon boarding, Yo had noticed an older man who appeared to be traveling alone, sitting across from him. About 90 minutes after they began riding the rails, the man startled Yoyo slightly by politely speaking to him:

"Are you going all the way to Beijing, son?" the man inquired.

"Yes sir, I am." Yoyo responded.

"Yes, that's good. It's a fascinating place full of history. Have you been many times before?"

"Never been there, not even once."

"Ahhh I see. Well you can expect to have a nice time then young man. Will you be staying long?"

"No, I am interviewing at Peking University on Tuesday!" Yoyo offered...with a degree of palpable excitement added to their conversation for the first time.

"That's a wonderful opportunity. Congratulations." said the man in the dark grey blazer and crisp white shirt.

Yoyo burst into a big smile.

"Yes, yes it is quite an opportunity."

Thirty minutes later, the two passengers, who had exchanged names by then, were still chatting. Yoyo had learned that the man, Li Jun, was a businessman who needed to attend meetings at Huawei for the upcoming week. Li Jun also disclosed that he was a graduate of Chengdu University, twenty years prior. Yoyo quickly ascertained that he was a man in his early 40s. Blurred images of China's landscape flew by them in a nanosecond, as the train reached speeds just north of 300 km/hour. The gentle hum of their car hurtling along the electrified rails below provided no real noise impediment, so the men continued their chat for almost two hours.

Yoyo was very open about his goals and his passion for language and cultural studies. He was comforted when Li Jun disclosed that he could indeed relate to Yoyo's circumstances, and the uncertainty of what was to come. Yoyo was usually a good judge of character. He noted that his new acquaintance was a kind and empathetic man. He savoured the interaction with this older well-dressed man and he felt like he was no longer alone as he embarked on his new life. Eventually, the rhythm of their conversation slowed considerably, and Li Jun said that he needed to get some sleep. He drifted off quickly, leaving Yoyo alone with his thoughts of his soon-to-be adventure to visit the University of his Dreams, as well as the bright lights and the modern skyscrapers of Beijing.

Hold on Tight

The train pulled into the western Beijing station shortly after 6:30 a.m. on Monday April 15th, in time for the businessmen and women aboard to have a productive day and attend their meetings. Before his trip Yoyo had reached out to a high school classmate from his hometown who was attending Peking U. Fortunately, his friend remembered Yoyo fondly, and made room in his small apartment for him to crash until his return trip on Thursday morning. Yoyo had decided to stay until Thursday as he had been told that the Admissions office provided a rejection or acceptance answer within 24 hours after all interviews. Evidently they had to focus on process efficiency since their office had to screen tens of thousands of applicants for every Master's program Peking University offered at that time. Indeed, as it turned out, they were ruthlessly efficient.

Staying there for three nights would also give Yoyo a chance to see Tiananmen Square and a few other historical sites that he yearned to see up close. Before he headed home he achieved that goal, and took dozens of photos to document his excursions in the city. His favourite sites in Beijing were the Square, the campus of Tsinghua, and the Temple of Heaven.

His panel format, on campus interview, was scheduled for 16:00 on Monday afternoon. The intense anxiety and occasional stomach churn that began on the train had not subsided. He truly believed that this opportunity was the chance of a lifetime so he arrived early; the interview started a few minutes past the top of the hour. Yoyo handled the first three questions well, although he still was not at ease. After mentioning that his favourite writer was Shakespeare, the panel members wanted to verify his passion for some of the classic tragedies. After he mixed up the main characters in Othello and Macbeth, Yoyo started to get a sinking feeling. He answered the last few questions well, but like Macbeth himself, a combination of hubris and ambition would lead to his downfall. Momentarily feeling overconfident, wanting to impress the interviewers and blinded by his ambitions, Yoyo ended up on a pathway he wasn't able to navigate in the darkness of his anxiety.

Just after noon the next day, as he finished his visit to Tiananmen Square, his cell phone buzzed. It was a number he did not recognize, but assumed it was likely Peking Admissions after he read the text message: "Hello, if you are able to take a call now please respond with Shi" *(translates to yes in English)*.

Minutes later, Yoyo's phone rang. His heart was racing faster than ever before as he waited for the voice on the other end to inform him of his fate. Without empathy and with a surgeon's precision, the caller told Yoyo that they were sorry, but he would not be receiving a position at Peking University. Speechless, he said absolutely nothing...and eventually dropped the phone at his feet with his mouth agape. Moments later, tears streamed down his face as he stood alone, thousands of kilometers from home, trying to process this terrible news.

Yoyo lost his appetite, so he skipped lunch and tried to continue his touring plans for the day. By midafternoon, he realized he felt like a zombie and he just wanted to go back to the apartment where he was staying that week. He decided he would cut his sightseeing short, and continue the next day. Fortunately, Yoyo was not a drinker, or he would have no doubt spent the rest of the day soothing his pain at one of the local bars. Instead, Yo took the subway back to his friend's place and hoped he would find him there so he could have a shoulder to cry on. Unfortunately, he arrived at an empty apartment until his friend returned just before the dinner hour. After speaking briefly with his childhood friend, an idea popped into Yo's mind....maybe he should call Mr. Tutu for consolation, and ask for his advice on what to do next. During the train ride he had thought several times about a script - the words he could use to surprise his mentor with this great achievement. Now he would be calling for a different reason, but Yoyo still had an overwhelming need to talk to Tutu at this difficult time.

He did not reach Mr. Tutu, but left his call back number. In the early evening the teacher and his protégé were able to connect, and had a lengthy conversation. It had been four years since he last saw Tutu, so he found the sound of his voice very soothing. One of the things Yo really admired about his teacher was his knowledge of philosophy and the wisdom he gleaned from Tutu. Incredibly, by the time Yoyo boarded the train back to Chengdu, his mindset was far more stoic, and even optimistic about finding another fulfilling pathway. Once again this older, influential man was able to provide Yo some happiness, providing a refuge from this big disappointment.

The return trip to Chengdu station was uneventful and Yoyo was back on campus and in his classes Friday morning. Although he hung on to the recent advice of his teacher/mentor, the next two weeks were difficult. Yoyo did his work, but without his usual enthusiasm and attention to detail. He continued to brainstorm other ideas, but to his credit, did not wallow in the pain of being rejected in Beijing.

One of Yoyo's classmates told him he would be attending the University job fair, to be held on the following Monday. One of the ideas percolating in his mind was to find a high pay, full time job, ending his studies. If he took that route, he would be able to assist his parents financially, easing their burdens. Maybe he could earn enough money so that they did not have to operate their booths selling in the streets anymore; maybe, just maybe, they could finally rest. In fact, as the job fair event approached, Yoyo was leaning in that direction more and more.

On that first Monday in May, dozens of employers came to Chengdu looking to meet the most motivated, soon-to-be graduates. Several Chinese-based businesses like Huawei and ZTE attended, but far bigger international businesses could be found there recruiting talent. Successful firms such as P&G, Microsoft, Motorola, Nokia, and Ericsson all opened booths and garnered much student interest. Yoyo, however, stopped at only one corporate booth, and briefly. In hindsight, sometimes our instincts and the unconscious mind help steer us away from "the road not taken", to quote the great poet Robert Frost. On that day, facing a fork in the road, a young man from rural China did indeed choose the road less traveled.

Near the back of the hall, Yoyo approached a booth backed by a remarkable image of the Himalayan Mountains. He wandered over and immediately had the full attention of the two staff manning the booth, since traffic at their location seemed to be light. He introduced himself and listened as the recruiters took turns telling Yoyo some of the benefits of studying and working in Tibet. They explained that one of the biggest staffing needs continued to be English instructors (who would also act as translators and tutors where necessary). Mainland Chinese perceived working in Tibet as mostly a missionary/volunteer type of career pathway; so fewer and fewer young people were willing and able to forego more enticing careers in the rapidly growing economy. Talented, bilingual people like Yoyo were very hard to find.

While listening to the recruiters, Yoyo became mildly intrigued, but needed time to process what he had heard, and to read the promotional brochure they gave to him. He thanked them and told them he would think about it, but made no commitments beyond that. As he sat on a nearby bench sipping on a tea he purchased, it became apparent that there would indeed be some nice benefits to working in

Tibet, the autonomous region of China, a place that so few had ever seen. He could satisfy his urge to study, and immerse himself into a new culture. Furthermore, he liked the thought of spending a year or two living in an idyllic place with a relatively quiet life, a place ripe with opportunity for contemplation and spiritual growth. He would be able to gain work experience, have the status of being a teacher like Tutu, and likely make important decisions about his career and his love life.

He decided he would return and pay the Tibetan recruiters another visit. Less than 30 minutes later, Yoyo was back at their booth, asking questions with the curiosity of a honey badger. He found out that Tibet University had less than 8,000 students, with small class sizes. He discovered that the ESL teaching job would most likely allow him ample free time to do that soul searching he believed necessary at this point in his life. This might work. So he then moved the needle and asked them: what type of hiring process were they using and how long would it take to know if they wanted to hire him?

After applying the very next day, Yoyo successfully interviewed with them two days later. And voila, without much delay, they decided that they had their man. It was obvious to the recruiters that Yoyo was a great fit for the profile of candidate they sought. They offered all new hires - and expected him to sign - a five year contract paying him $200US monthly. He put pen to paper, without hesitation.

June of 2002 was the time for graduation and many good-byes at Chengdu U. In Yoyo's case he was now considered a true scholar. He received a huge honour when his graduation paper was chosen as the best of all submitted within the Faculty of Foreign Languages. That honour entitled Yoyo to attend a prestigious conference in mid-June where other winners from all other disciplines gather annually to present their research/thesis to a large panel of professors from all Chengdu faculties. Yoyo presented his findings regarding cross-cultural teaching. The professors were very impressed. He received praise and a compilation grade of 9.5 on a scale of 10. His time as an undergraduate finished with a flourish, and only three months after the biggest disappointment of his young life, Yoyo was exuberant once again.

Like so many students in China, Aki and Yoyo viewed the summer after graduation as the best chance to do a special trip. Although some grads went abroad, they decided to travel in China - using the money they had saved from their bursaries. They decided to take a cruise on the Yangtze (Chang Jiang) River. Their plan was that at the conclusion of the cruise Yoyo would be able to take his best friend to see his hometown, and meet his immediate family. Aki would then return briefly to his home province mid-summer, before embarking on his new plan and starting his job in Beijing. So after a few days of research and asking agents for recommendations, Yoyo found a good option - they could tour together for seven days towards his home province on a ship from Chongqing east to Jiangxi, where he grew up. They bought their tickets on the last Friday in June and then climbed aboard the boat on July 3rd.

As the boys had imagined, the long and winding Yangtze River was a sight to behold, full of surprises and beautiful but ragged riverside landscapes. From its source in the high mountains of Tibet, to its mouth at the East China Sea near Shanghai, it runs for almost 6,300 km. The Yangtze passes through three large gorges in central China. During their voyage, adjacent to those gorges, Yoyo and Aki were able to see many hanging coffins of some Chinese minority groups. Certain pockets of Chinese ancestors used to hang the coffins of their relatives off the cliffs of the gorges. Apparently they did so as sort of an everlasting tribute, so their family members could be visible to all cargo and cruise ship passengers.

Fortunately, at that time the Chinese government had not yet approved and began construction on The Three Gorges Dam; a massive hydroelectricity project along the Yangtze. So this was one final chance for the two friends to see the river in its pristine form, prior to the intrusions of human development. From Yoyo's perspective, he noted that the diverse widths of the river (with the varied speeds of the current) represent the various stages of life - fast paced at times, calmer and slower at other times. He spent a lot of time wondering which of those paces he would find in Tibet. He was excited to get home and tell his parents about this awesome experience.

Yoyo's parents were eager to see their son again, and happy to meet Yoyo's best friend. Aki stayed in the family home for six days and they slept together in Yoyo's bedroom. Those five nights would probably be the last time the two friends, confidants, and occasional lovers would be together, but they decided to keep their nights as platonic as possible out of respect for the Yan family. While they were not sleeping in the closet, they stayed in the metaphorical one.

Aki and Yoyo shared memories, fears, laughter and dreams that week. They were drifting between joy and melancholy, since they were fully aware that they would soon be heading in separate directions.

Not long after that the day of Aki's departure was upon them. The boys went to the Nanchang Railway Station together early that morning so Aki could catch the 7:30 a.m. train heading north. While waiting on the platform they bid one another a very emotional, tearful farewell. When Aki noticed Yoyo's tears, he came to him and began to console him by gently rubbing his back, and said clear and comforting words that Yoyo would remember forever: "Don't cry Yoyo. Don't cry". Waves of admiration and love overwhelmed Yoyo, but he could not speak. He spent the next few weeks regretting his inability to say how he felt, but on some level he believed that Aki knew anyway.

Hold on Tight

Chapter 6 *Teaching in Tibet*

At the beginning of September Yoyo Yan arrived in Lhasa, Tibet's capital city. He soon learned that Tibet is also known as the "Roof of the World". He was now living more than 2,000 kilometers west of his home province at an altitude of over 4,000 meters above sea level. He was employed at an academic institution, known as Tibet University. He was a teacher. He was a translator. He was also on a five year commitment to his new employer. Only the last part scared him.

Life in Tibet was, as he expected, quite different. But that was sort of the point. Yoyo was curious, fascinated even, with cultural variances, and he could not think of a better culture contrast within China than Tibetan culture. Pilgrimages to sacred mountains and lakes, yearning for enlightenment, creating karma, and showing unrestrained allegiance to religious leaders from centuries past are all part of locals daily life in this city. One day before his courses got too busy he decided he would visit the World Heritage site called the Potala Palace, a massive and immensely impressive building wedged into the side of Marpo Ri (Red Hill) on the northern edge of the Himalayan mountain range. The palace functioned as the winter palace for the Dalai Lamas for 300 years beginning in the mid-1600s. The leader of the Buddhist faith, the aforementioned Dalai Lama, also governed the region until the Chinese central government took control of Tibet in 1959. According to Buddhist beliefs, the current Dalai Lama is a reincarnation of a deceased lama who decided to be reborn again to continue his important work.

Hold on Tight

Reincarnation is a fundamental tenet of Buddhist faith, but the belief in the ongoing cycle of life is not the one that Yoyo embraced halfway through his first year at Tibet University. Instead, he decided to follow the vegan diet espoused by the Buddhists. Although it is not banned outright, meat is considered unnecessary, excessive and unjustifiable. Yoyo began consuming a diet of mainly rice or noodles, soy and wheat gluten based foods like tofu and tempeh, and whatever limited vegetables that became available in that particular season. Near the end of his first year, he invited his parents to visit him, making the lengthy bus trip due west from Qinghai province. His parents, still being carnivores and eating as much meat as they could afford to, were very upset when they observed Yo's constrained, vegan diet. Yoyo had lost more than 10 pounds in the eight months since that previous summer, though he felt great. His parents at first encouraged, and finally pleaded with Yoyo to reverse his vegetarian lifestyle, but to no avail. He ate no meat while living in Tibet.

As an English teacher, Yoyo was extremely motivated and selfless. His students' needs always came before his own, and as a new teacher, he needed to be very dedicated to lesson planning. At the end of his first year, Yoyo was even chosen as one of the best teachers by his students (who were almost the same age as he was at 20-23 years old). Meanwhile, several students who adored him requested songs to be played over the public address system at the school on special occasions. His self-confidence was flourishing. He eventually came to realize that working in Tibet, while again not his first choice, proved to be a good decision.

Tibetan instructors, much like most fully tenured professors, are expected to write research papers. Yoyo's third teaching paper on cross-cultural teaching became a ticket for a much needed working vacation. He got invited to present it at a university English teaching forum in Beijing where ESL teachers gather annually from across China to share and learn from one another. Meanwhile, Yoyo had very little communication with Aki since Yo was so isolated. Consequently, Aki purchased an Ericsson phone and mailed it across the country for Yoyo to use. Yo had never owned a mobile phone before. It was the size and density of a small brick, but it was a thoughtful and very useful gift that arrived just in time for Chinese New Year, 2003. For the first time in his life, Yoyo slowly became more adept at SMS (text) messages. His relationship with Aki was once again on his mind frequently. So in May of 2003 Yoyo sent this text to Aki:

Aki honey, I have been invited to visit Beijing in August! I will accept. Please tell me you will be at home during that week.

Aki's reply brought a smile to his face that lasted for days.

My dear that is wonderful news. I will try to be here for you. Please tell me the dates when you know them.

Meanwhile, although it was infrequent, Yoyo continued to keep in touch with Mr. Tutu, who was still teaching at the high school back home in Shanggao. Shortly after delivering the good news about his second opportunity to visit the country's capital, he called Mr. Tutu to inform him. Much to Yoyo's delight, Mr. Tutu said he was also planning a trip to Beijing that summer to see some family. Additionally, Tutu offered that he would try to coordinate the dates of his trip so that they would be in the capital simultaneously. Yoyo was absolutely ecstatic. He thought about a recent lesson he taught his students, inspired by Confucian beliefs:

When three are walking together, I am sure to find teachers among them. I will select their good qualities and follow those, and observe their bad qualities and avoid those - Confucius

Hold on Tight

The faculty supervisor in the Foreign Languages School where Yoyo was working wrote to him by email and told him that the University would be flying him to Beijing for five days, departing August 16. She told Yoyo that accommodations would be provided for him at the Beijing Foreign Studies University campus hostel. The conference he would be attending was August 18 and 19th, with his presentation scheduled for the morning of Tuesday the 19th. She told him that her administrative assistant would be handling the flight details and she would be in touch to finalize the trip in 14 days. Yoyo mulled this over, and gave the information to Mr. Tutu and to Aki as he waited for the itinerary to be finalized on Sichuan Airlines.

Armed with more self-confidence after a successful year teaching, and given that no classes were in session until early September, Yoyo replied to his supervisor with a request: could he stay longer in Beijing if he found his own accommodations after his stay at the hostel ended? She responded affirmatively, and provided her assistant's contact information so that he could work out the return flight with her directly. After reaching her assistant the next day, Yoyo worked with her to arrange an August 26 flight back to Lhasa. That Tuesday return flight was actually less expensive, so his request worked out for everyone. He was anticipating the extension would allow him, Aki and possibly even Mr. Tutu to spend an entire weekend together after the conference; but only if they could coordinate their schedules. That evening, Yoyo shared the dates with Aki and Tutu, and hoped for the best.

Chapter 7 *The Philosophers*

O n the third day of August, Yoyo received a call from Mr. Tutu. His old teacher told him that he was able to arrange his trip to Beijing so as to be free on the weekend following Yoyo's conference. He said he was looking forward to getting caught up. Tutu told Yoyo he would go ahead and arrange a hotel with two beds and a rollaway bed so that the three of them could be together and would have a comfortable place to stay. Remembering Yoyo's zeal for learning and self-development, he suggested Yoyo borrow some books from the university library to keep him busy on his flight across the country. His mentor recommended a few titles in particular, written by a few of his favourite philosophers:

A Discourse of the Arts & Sciences by Jean-Jacques Rousseau

Experience & Education by John Dewey

The Republic by Plato

An Essay Concerning Human Understanding & Two Treatises of Government by John Locke

Yoyo had already studied parts of The Republic while at Chengdu, so he decided to look for something written by John Locke instead. With only two weeks until he left for Beijing, he went to the library and got busy. He started reading Rousseau first, finishing it in five days. The Dewey book was more challenging, a bit more of a slog, and he managed to read about 150 pages in the days before he left. Yoyo was determined that, if he was only going to see Mr.

Tutu one more time, he would be ready to make the most of the experience. He started devouring Locke the night before his flight, and fell asleep with the book laying on his chest and the lamp in full glow.

Sichuan flight 909 arrived at the Beijing Capital Airport slightly late, just after 18:00 on August 16. Yoyo was getting anxious as he waited for his checked bag, as he knew Aki was waiting in the terminal for him. It had been a full year apart, and Yoyo missed his best friend. Texting multiple times each week helped bridge the divide, but it was no substitute for hearing his comforting baritone voice and seeing his imperfect, yet heartwarming smile. Finally, he emerged from the secure area, and when the sliding doors opened Yoyo was stunned to see a colourful throng of people of all ages, sizes, and genders staring at him. He thought, am I on stage here? Is this how a musician feels when the curtain opens and he or she first sees their audience? It was a fleeting thought, and then his focus quickly turned to finding Aki's face in the sea of people. Yoyo jostled his way through the impatient crowd for at least 10 minutes, but eventually found Aki near the back of the gathering. They embraced briefly, firmly...before letting go and heading for the exit.

August in Beijing is usually hot and quite crowded with Chinese nationals who have come home from their endeavors all over the world. That summer was no exception. It was at least 15 degrees warmer than the weather he left behind in the Himalayan Mountains, and Yoyo was caught by surprise. He wasn't sure he had clothing suitable for the summer heat, but he didn't care. He was just thrilled to visit the capital for the second time, and for the first time with his first love. The young men found a taxi and headed for Aki's apartment, located about 6 km north of Tiananmen Square. Given the long day Yoyo was expecting on Monday, they decided to order food delivered and share a bottle of special wine that Aki had chilling in his small fridge. Excursions around the city could wait. Fortunately, they knew that there would be six days after the conference for fun. Just before 23:00 Yoyo jumped into a cab and headed for the university hostel where his bed for the next three nights awaited.

He stayed up well past midnight on Sunday night, rehearsing some of the more difficult elements of his presentation. Yo felt at peace knowing he would only be listening and asking questions as an attendee on the first day. He would have another full day to prepare for his contribution to the educators' conference. The Monday morning sunrise arrived quickly after a short but deep sleep. No time for breakfast, but Yoyo knew the hosts would provide some food on site. He checked his inbox to find the address and walking directions to the Norman Bethune Auditorium. He was surprised, but happy to see a note from Mr. Tutu, who was waiting for him. It was an email he had sent to Yoyo the previous evening. He glanced at it briefly, and the tone was affirmative and the content mentioned a hotel name and potentially getting together Friday. Reading the details and replying would have to wait. Yoyo wanted to be on time for the 8:30 registration and the 9:00 start. He left just before 8:00, and arrived on time.

The English teachers from all over China were thoughtful and dedicated. The keynote speaker was excellent and well prepared. Yoyo made many mental and physical notes, and grew excited to apply some of his learning when he returned to teach his upcoming classes. After day one concluded, he went out for dinner with a new acquaintance from a Hong Kong school, then returned to his room to reply to Mr. Tutu and prepare for his presentation the next morning. He told Tutu that the plans made for two nights at the Crowne Plaza Wangfujing hotel were fine and suggested they meet in the lobby midafternoon on Friday.

Yoyo remained hopeful that Aki would be able to join them. He told Tutu he would get back to him again later with an exact meet up time.

While day two of the conference was also informative, after Yoyo finished his 20 minute presentation he found his mind adrift throughout the rest of the day. He was anticipating what might follow in the days ahead. He thought about one of the most transformational things he learned from Mr. Tutu, a lesson in his senior year that included a profound piece of wisdom from Soren Kierkegaard:

"Life can only be understood backwards; but it must be lived forwards."

Kierkegaard's message resonated with Yoyo. It would linger in his mind, and although he did not realize it in the summer of 2003, it would be a catalyst for more change to come very soon.

That Tuesday evening, and the next two days that followed were unstructured time, allowing Yoyo a sense of freedom he rarely felt. He moved out of the university based hostel and spent some quality time with Aki, who had taken Thursday and Friday off work. He continued to read Locke when Aki was busy, and used Aki's desktop computer to read some interesting philosophies on the internet. It was a joyous time, and he expected the week would get even better when they met up with his mentor. The plans were all set - the three of them would meet up at the hotel Friday at 3:00 pm.

The Crowne Plaza is a nice, budget friendly, four star hotel situated in the heart of Wangfujing's shopping district. It has over 300 rooms, all on the perimeter of a stunning atrium with an elevated platform holding a grand piano for added evening ambiance. They got there before 3:00, but it appeared Tutu had not yet arrived; so the two friends took the opportunity to wander around, admiring the scale and the many amenities of the hotel. A four star hotel was a new frontier for Yoyo. After a few minutes they found seats near the unoccupied piano, and just enjoyed the view. Yoyo had a mental flashback of the small, three room home he grew up in with Meiying and their parents; and while that imagery was completely unexpected, his face changed into a wide smile when he pondered how far he had come.

Mr. Tutu arrived shortly before 3:15, and found his former student, waiting for him in the atrium. After exchanging warm greetings, the trio went to the front desk to check in and ensure the room was equipped properly to sleep three. The clerk who processed their arrival and took payment from Mr. Tutu told them that their room was ready and a rollaway bed would be delivered to them that evening. The polite porter carried their luggage, and showed them to their room.

Room 833 was larger than expected, with high ceilings that made it look even more spacious. There were two large beds and a small seating area with two red, arc backed chairs. Yoyo took a peek into the bathroom and could not believe his eyes. On the beautiful faux granite counter he saw an alluring arrangement of Borghese-branded shampoo, conditioner, body wash, cleanser, hydrating emulsion and two bars of soap. His femininity had inadvertently surfaced. This luxurious room would be their home for the next 48 hours, and it felt like a slice of heaven to the young man from the village of Guoyuanchang.

After unpacking, the three of them decided to spend some time in the atrium, talking over a pot of tea. To start, the conversation began with stories of Tibet, Beijing, and then a few of Mr. Tutu's recent classroom anecdotes. Yoyo had thought long and hard about whether he should and could bring up the topic of sexuality during their time with

Tutu, to openly inquire and learn about that seemingly taboo topic for the first time in his life. He thought it best to steer clear of mentioning it, unless he and his mentor found themselves alone for a period of time. It would likely be too awkward otherwise. If sexuality came up naturally, he decided he would roll with it and do more listening than speaking. However, as it turned out, the weekend was full of discussions and interpretations of various philosophers and how to live a more fulfilling, moral life; just as Yoyo had hoped. He knew his time with Mr. Tutu was limited, and his goal was to learn as much as possible.

Yoyo asked Tutu about the concept of empiricism. There is little doubt that some educators and their pupils may not fully agree with, or totally understand empiricism... but Mr. Tutu was not one of them. He reached deep inside his massive vault of a mind, and shared two of John Locke's thoughts on experiential learning:

"The mind is furnished with ideas by experience alone"
– Locke

Actually experiencing the world through our own 5 senses is the only way to truly know something
– Locke, paraphrased

That led to a long discussion about destiny, experiential learning, educational pedagogy, and the value of interpersonal relationships and travel. Skillfully, Tutu decided to challenge his companions with a question....

"Boys if you could only do one, is it best to learn about the mechanics of literature and forms of poetry by attending a lecture, or is it better to be steered toward reading great prose and set free to craft your own voice by putting pen to paper?"

From reading Locke, Yoyo knew the answer, and he was glad his instincts were being validated by Tutu's articulate challenge. Tutu then asked them if they were familiar with the Roman stoic named Seneca the Younger. After pausing to search his memory, Aki offered that he thought Seneca was a believer in the Latin phrase *carpe diem* / seize the day. Tutu confirmed Aki's statement as he carefully refilled their tea cups and then his own. He paused, and then went on to say that Seneca was a proponent of embracing each day as a learning opportunity:

"We are always complaining that our days are few, and acting as though there would be no end of them" - Seneca

He let that quotation linger for a few moments, and then he smiled and said this as an extension of Seneca's wisdom:

"Associate with people who are likely to improve you" - Seneca

When that discussion ended, they discussed a plan for their evening meal. They asked the concierge for dinner recommendations and he suggested they try the Peking duck at Siji Minfu Restaurant in the Dongcheng district. Their weekend was just getting started, and Yoyo was already enjoying himself immensely. They went to change clothing and then hailed a cab as slivers of the late day sun shimmered between the skyscrapers.

Over dinner, Aki told his companions about what he liked about living in Beijing, and Mr. Tutu mentioned some of the things he had enjoyed over the years while visiting his family there. All of that confirmed what Yoyo already knew - that one day he needed to live there and heed Locke's advice. He hoped that after his contract in Tibet he could find work and in the booming capital. That dream would allow him to extend his resume, while simultaneously advancing his relationship with Aki - maybe they could even live together, cook together, and sleep together?

After enjoying the duck and some dumplings, the trio did some window shopping in the Wangfujing district. Much of what they saw was priced far beyond their means, so it did not take long for Yoyo to suggest another idea. He was much more interested in spending time continuing their discussions of the great philosophers - and much more focused on how he might be able to find clues in their wisdom that could shape his future. He was no doubt inspired by one of the greatest Greek philosophers:

"The unexamined life is not worth living" – Socrates

Yoyo asked his companions if they would like to conclude their evening with some more conversation in a local bar, while sharing a bottle of wine. Tutu welcomed the idea, as he wasn't a shopper and not at all a materialistic man. Aki was less enthusiastic about that idea, but agreed to it when Yoyo persuaded him with a deft reference to something he had learned in Tibet:

"Aki we must keep in mind what Confucius said":

"Time flows away like the water in a river"

Mr. Tutu smiled warmly and told Yoyo that was one of his favorite quotes from the old Chinese philosopher. He added that the veracity of time being a scarce resource was one of the reasons he adjusted his personal schedule to be able to meet up with his younger protégé. When you get to be a certain age, time really does become one's currency; and apparently Mr. Tutu was at that age. It was becoming clear to all that this August rendezvous was a great idea.

Just before 21:00 they discovered Mo Bar, an establishment that was less than half full, so they agreed to hang out there for the remainder of the evening. They mapped out a rough idea about their next day's itinerary, their only one full day together. They ultimately decided that they wanted to visit the Forbidden City and learn more about Chinese history.

The three of them slept separately and as well as could be expected in a new environment Friday night, although Yoyo had a bit of trouble finding comfort on the narrow, uncomfortable cot. He rousted the others the next morning, and they prepared for their excursions. They were still having thoughtful discussions about life and love and morality, but the topic of human sexuality never came up. On two separate occasions Yoyo found an opportunity to steer the conversation in that direction, but he was too timid. Finally, later that day, after the trio had returned from their touring. Aki decided he needed some time alone so he took a nap.

Yoyo took advantage of being with Tutu alone and asked him what he thought of Sigmund Freud's work. Although he waited and wanted to see how Tutu reacted to the mention of Freud's name before getting down into the weeds, Yoyo actually wanted to discuss a very specific and controversial Freudian claim. He was hoping to discern whether or not Tutu agreed that it is possible that all humans are born bisexual, and were nurtured into becoming straight or gay by their important early relationships, and possibly even their life experiences. If Tutu seemed open to that rather radical theory it could create a window for young Yoyo to disclose his own attractions and figure out what they meant exactly. He was mostly at ease, since he could think of nobody more thoughtful and less judgmental than Tutu that he could speak to about this difficult topic.

Somewhat apologetically, Tutu responded that he was not that familiar with Freud's research, and not at all familiar with his views on sexual preferences. Yoyo demurred, then took a different tact. He asked his mentor if he thought homosexuality was an illness, something that could be "cured" like a cancer. His teacher said that view was popular amongst older generations but likely misguided. He went on to say that he did not know any gay people himself, so he was not that familiar with their values or lifestyle.

After about 10 seconds of silence, Tutu continued by quietly and respectfully asking Yoyo why he was so interested in that topic. Yoyo noted the change of voice tone, and sensed he may have indeed found a sympathetic ear - this might be his chance to have a confidant. He decided that he would stay quiet about his truth for now, but might share his attractions to men with Tutu at some later time. Instead of revealing his truth Yoyo told Tutu that he had a close friend back in Tibet who was questioning his sexuality, and had come to him for counsel. Closeted gays view lying as an unfortunate necessity. Deception is a difficult habit to break.

Later in the evening, Yoyo went up to the room to check on Aki. He waited for his buddy to finish showering, and then they went back downstairs to join Tutu. They spent the remainder of their final evening together chatting in the atrium and enjoying the soothing sounds of the talented weekend pianist. The three of them spent time discussing Rousseau and Socrates. That evening, combined with the whole weekend, validated that Yo's attraction to older men was deeply rooted in intellectual stimulation; apparently more so than any physical desire. After so many confusing years, his understanding of his own sexuality and attractions was beginning to crystallize.

Chapter 8 *Restless in the Himalayas*

Yoyo flew back to Tibet on August 26, 2003. His return flight was uneventful; however his trip to Beijing was anything but. He was returning home with some educational best practices from the conference, but more importantly he now possessed a mental clarity that made him feel a few inches taller. Although he knew he would miss Aki, he was looking forward to the beginning of a new school year. Classes began September 3rd, and teacher Yan was full of energy and new ideas.

Yoyo made one change to his lesson planning that proved to be particularly effective. He built in more peer editing time, more collaboration in the classroom. He encouraged his students to correct each other's work, suggesting improvements. He then collected and assessed the edited pieces of writing, and rewarded not only the best pieces, but also acknowledged their editors when they had made great suggestions. In his second year he also realized that some students needed a second opportunity to revise something they submitted, if they misunderstood the expectations or were otherwise underperforming. He referred to that revision policy as "mastery" learning. His students continued to respond, achieve and perform for him.

In the autumn of that second year Yoyo began to accept his same-sex attractions, although he was still not comfortable being labelled as homosexual, gay, queer or any of the other more disparaging terms some people use.

For some LGBTQ folks, especially younger people, those labels can make one feel inferior, even defective. While attitudes about same-sex relationships were shifting marginally in China's metropolises, Tibet was another story. Buddhist monks held firm with the belief in Kama Sutta, that those people who give into sensual temptations will endure emotional (and sometimes physical) pain and suffering.

The Buddha himself said this:

"So one, always mindful, should avoid sensual desires. Letting them go, he will cross over the flood like one who, having bailed out the boat, has reached the far shore."

Yoyo was certainly not a member of the monastery during his time teaching in Tibet, nor was he a practicing Buddhist. But when immersed in a culture that yearns for purity and the discipline to resist erotic pleasures, the paradox of 'coming out' while also avoiding sex was very tough to reconcile. As Yo wrestled with this incongruity, he wondered how he could explore his sexuality/seek a male companion and simultaneously not be condemned by the University administration, amongst others. He decided he would do two things at that time. He would read more about life and love, and he would take an excursion to Mount Everest.

In October of his second year in Tibet, Yoyo read Sogyal Rinpoche's The Tibetan Book of Living and Dying, which is a fascinating book that helps the reader understand human existence. The power of Rinpoche's wisdom was actually not completely related to preparing for one's death; rather it focuses on how one can live a more fulfilling life so that the anxiety about one's inevitable death is turned upside down. Pondering and being prepared for death, according to the author, offers tremendous hope for a human being. Additionally, some of the most enlightening (and enduring) understandings Yoyo took from Rinpoche were and continue to be:

→ Learn How to Relax (and use nature to help you accomplish this)
→ Seek Enlightenment/Know Yourself
→ Accept & Embrace Impermanence
→ Meditate to Unknot the Mind

Shortly after finishing the book, Yoyo found time to visit historic Lake Namtso. One of the other Tibet University faculty members, Hong, told him about the lake over lunch one day. Hong was a woman in her early 30s, about ten years older than Yo. Standing tall at 177 cm, she was slightly taller than Yoyo, which was quite unusual. He wasn't sure he knew any women who were taller than him; and if he did he certainly couldn't name one. Hong had dark eyes that seemed to light up when she talked about some aspects of Chinese history and her Buddhist beliefs. Her clothing of preference were revealing silk camisoles, usually white but sometimes more colourful. Although he had never been intimate with a woman, he noted that his colleague was quite attractive. She was also clearly a historian with a zest for life and adventure.

Since he had just read so much about using nature to relax and find enlightenment, he was searching for new opportunities to do just that. He asked her more about why so many others do pilgrimages to that spot, and if she had ever been there before. Hong informed Yoyo that it was a sacred lake; which fortunately was located only about two hundred kilometers from their university in Lhasa. Many Buddhists believed Lake 'Nam' to be the neighbour to heaven, mainly due to its elevation nestled inside snow-capped mountains, the Lake's pristine blue water, and because of its associations with important spirits. Hong went on to say that she had been there before, but still wanted to go a third time with a tourist group, possibly on the last Sunday in October. She almost insisted that Yoyo join her. She was trying to impress and stimulate his mind so she could get a look at her colleague's body. Intrigued by her delightful descriptions, but somewhat put off by her boldness, Yoyo wavered and simply said he was busy with his teaching but would contact her if he was available to go. Eventually he relented and agreed to join them. When the group arrived at Lake Nam Yoyo was blown away. He agreed with this new friend – Nam was exactly what total tranquility feels like; so full of life under the water yet so tranquil on the surface.

Yoyo's subsequent decision to check out Mount Everest base camp was also made with the objective of using nature to relax. What he didn't realize before the trip was that he would have an opportunity to meditate, to "unknot" his mind. Unexpectedly, while meditating at that altitude he intimately sensed an afterlife for the first time in his 24 years. To those of us who have been fortunate enough to feel the presence of "heaven" or some version of the afterlife; we know that this experience is often transformative. So many humans live on Earth wondering about death and what, if anything, happens after our last breath. Believing that an afterlife exists affects different people in different ways. Yoyo was able to accept our shared impermanence, so he felt lighter and free to fly.

After returning to Lhasa from his excursions to Lake Namtso & Everest and after losing his bicycle in a dreadfully snowy winter, Yoyo fully realized and accepted that Tibet was not his ultimate destination. It was just one station on a long journey. He knew he needed to use John Locke's advice; and try to create even more sensory experiences. His sexuality was no longer as big a mystery nor a heavy burden to him, so he was yearning for some new experiences in a more gay-friendly environment.

"My religion is to live and die without regret." Milarepa

Yoyo really loved what Milarepa, the 11th century Tibetan had written, and he wondered what life would be like if he could be true to himself. Living without regret meant, ironically enough, that he would need to leave Tibet. Yoyo was beginning to think that if he found a tolerant and progressive country to live in maybe he could actually get married and start a family with another man, living and dying without regret.

Consequently, after about five weeks of investigating his options, in April of 2004 Yoyo applied to do a Master's Degree in Norway, at Oslo University. They offered qualified students a one year Masters scholarship to study cross-cultural communications - a program that he thought was perfectly suited for his academic passions. However, it was not to be; another admissions disappointment was looming. After much planning and preparation for his new life in Europe, that exciting plan was undone by immigration authorities. Yoyo Yan's visa was denied. He was not going to get to meet *Thor* after all.

Yoyo finished the academic year, but was feeling very restless. He could not fulfill his commitment to three additional years at Tibet University. In late June, well before the third year of his contract began, Yoyo quit his teaching position there. He needed to follow the ongoing magnetic pull to Beijing. Unconsciously, his deep love for and attraction to Aki was still lingering in his mind. He felt a mixture of freedom, hope and anxiety about the uncertain road ahead.

Chapter 9 *Finally, Beijing*

After spending some time with Meiying and his parents that summer, Yoyo packed up a small suitcase and headed for the capital. His communication with Aki was more sporadic during August, but Yoyo understood that Aki was busy with his job. He was spending time getting ready for his move, so not particularly bothered by the silence. What Yo didn't realize was how much time Aki was spending with his girlfriend. Ak had kept that a secret. Regardless, Yoyo was pleased that he had an offer to stay in his buddy's small, one bedroom apartment until he could find his footing and earn an income. He was excited, anticipating that they would finally share a bed together....with full privacy.

Yoyo was certainly not going to be the first person to seek a new start in life, relocating to pursue a love interest. But it was a first for him. During the train ride to Beijing, Yo's mind was awash with tender moments from their time as undergraduates, two years prior. He thought about all the things he loved about Aki, and how his smile made Yoyo feel. He envisioned his new life in Beijing and wondered if he and Aki would get engaged. Would they be able to have a "marriage" with a civil ceremony, and how long would that take to become a possibility? How many children could they have? What would their names be? Yo's heart and mind were full of hope.

He arrived to begin this new chapter in Beijing in the early evening of September 2nd, 2004. Once again, his first love was waiting for h n. On that first night in Beijing, Yoyo had romance on his mind, and a few surprises for his friend and host. He decided that they would have a quick dinner at KFC, and then as a surprise, Yoyo would take Aki to a famous bakery (面包店) to treat him to his favourite dessert, caramel cheesecake. Yo envisioned that after they shared tea and dessert, if he was feeling brave enough, he would take another leap of faith. He would finally ask Aki to be his boyfriend.

Back in Chengdu, one of the many ways that Aki showed his affection for his smaller friend was by picking him up and carrying him on his back; the whimsical "piggyback ride". After leaving the bakery and when they were mostly alone, Yoyo deftly moved into position behind Aki just as he used to, clearly looking to be carried. After some hesitation and a little bit of prodding from Yoyo, Aki lifted Yo onto his back and they did this somewhat intimate dance from their past. Almost immediately, Aki turned his head towards Yoyo slightly, and proceeded to whisper something that crushed Yoyo's spirit.

"My friend, this will be the last time I carry you on my back."

Yoyo tried to enjoy the short ride, but he dismounted as soon as other pedestrians approached. A chilly silence suddenly pierced the hot September evening. Evidently the boyfriend suggestion would have to wait. Upon arrival back at Aki's apartment, the ice was broken as Yoyo was given a brief tour of the layout. Yoyo learned he would indeed be sleeping in Aki's bedroom, so some fleeting optimism returned. However, he could not get Aki's "last time" words out of his mind, but he knew he would have more opportunity to ask him about them later when the lights went out.

After Yoyo showered and prepared for bed, he was hoping for a warm embrace, a kiss, and maybe more. He dressed provocatively, in a tight, white t-shirt and his sexy new black and red jockstrap. He then eventually returned to the living area, where Aki was busy adding bed sheets to cover the couch. Momentarily confused, he paused and then asked what his host was doing.

"I'm just making up my bed Yoyo. I am letting you sleep in my bed."

Yoyo became very emotional. He said nothing. He left the room hastily and sat on Aki's bed trying to make sense of it all....the limited communication in August, the final piggyback, and the separate sleeping decision. He felt strange sensations in his chest - as though his lungs were collapsing. He sat in the darkened room, staring at his feet, distraught and without a clue what he should do next. Some 10 minutes later, Aki gently knocked on the door and cracked it part way open, to find his friend re-packing his toiletries into the mesh lining of his small suitcase.

"What are you doing Yoyo? Where are you going?" asked a puzzled Aki.

"Aki, I cannot be alone tonight."

"But....well you are not alone Yo. I will be here sleeping in the living room if you need me."

"That is not what I want, Aki. You can have your bed. I will leave and find another place to stay."

Aki, who was starting to understand the full picture, slowly retreated to the living area. He momentarily considered changing his plan and sleeping with Yoyo, but decided it wasn't his preference. Rather, he was seeking to simplify things so as to not feel any guilt, and not feel as if he was cheating on his girlfriend. Yoyo emerged after a few more minutes, with misty eyes and a dour demeanour. Aki rose to his feet and hugged Yoyo, but Yoyo quickly pulled himself away. His hopes and dreams for romance were obviously not becoming reality.

Since it was approaching midnight, he would have to find other accommodations, and fast. He asked Aki if he could spend a few more minutes in the apartment and got on his cell phone. Yoyo sent a text to a childhood friend named Wei. Fortunately, he responded. While Wei was clearly surprised by the urgency of the request, Wei was very pleased to hear from his old friend. He provided his address and told Yoyo he would stay up and wait for his arrival. Yoyo arrived at Wei's apartment at 1:15 a.m.

While living with Wei in the Beigao neighborhood, Yoyo spent his days trying to block out the pain of his first night in Beijing and the dashed dream of a life with Aki. He focused on searching for a job. Although it was not easy at times, especially late at night when he was alone with his thoughts, Yoyo was able to persevere, to move forward. He was grateful he could rely on a lesson he had taught to his students in Tibet; Niebuhr's serenity quote about accepting what he could not change. Yoyo only had one more phone conversation with Aki in those next few weeks....and it was not as emotional as he had feared. He learned that Aki was not comfortable with living his life any way but straight. Aki said he had been very distraught about encountering so much outside pressure to conform; and he endured many sleepless nights. He had started a relationship with a young woman, a woman he believed had the potential to be a great mother to his children. Yoyo listened intently and said very little as Aki explained his angst, and shed light on his chilly behaviour on that fateful night when Yoyo arrived.

After that final conversation, and especially after thinking about Aki's dilemma, Yoyo began to think differently. He felt a tinge of empathy, minor disappointment, and even feelings of relief when he came to realize that Aki was not able to process and apply some of the same philosophical wisdom that they had discussed only one year earlier, with Mr. Tutu. The empathy emanated from knowing how intense family and social pressures to conform, to have a traditional life, and to embrace a traditional family unit can be. His parents were expecting those things too; but Yoyo was still fighting to hold onto his new mantra: *to live and die without regrets.* The disappointment he felt needs not much explanation; he had lost his first love. He would now have to find someone else who returned his love in kind. The relief Yoyo felt was the hardest emotion to understand and reconcile. Eventually, he realized that his sense of relief had derived from being pleased that Aki might have found peace with his situation, may actually have found love, and that they would both be able to wake up and experience many more sunrises.

"Each morning we are born again. It is today that matters the most." - Buddha

Armed with his life experiences, his philosophies, and a broken relationship scar, Yoyo was able to shift his focus to his other goals during that period in the fall of 2004. He had a comfortable place to live temporarily, and a kind host in Wei. To keep the peace, he had not shared any of his Aki related dreams and subsequent disappointments with his family back in Jiangxi province, even Meiying. In fact, he called his family less often during that time. He knew his mother was usually a perceptive woman, and even over the phone she would likely realize that Yoyo was having a tough time. Therefore, he thought it best to wait until he found work and moved into his own place to live before resuming regular communication with them.

He was still in that mindset, when suddenly one day in mid-October his father called. Usually it was either Yoyo or his mother that initiated their calls, so his dad's call got Yoyo's attention. His father made some rather weak attempts at small talk at first, and when that subsided he asked Yoyo what historical locations he had seen so far in the capital city. While Yoyo rattled a few of the sites off to his father, a thought suddenly popped into his mind…'if father could take the time off work, maybe he could come to visit me here in Beijing?'

Chapter 10 *Finding Firm Footing*

W hile he certainly appreciated being given a place to stay while he got his feet beneath him, the bedroom he was given in Wei's flat was small and lifeless. There were no real disputes over space or house habits while the two lived together, but Yoyo noted that Wei seemed to become more subdued over the next few weeks. Additionally, Wei's apartment was not close to the bustling university campus where so many people in their twenties congregated and networked for their careers. Consequently, after almost three weeks of living in the Beigao district, Yoyo decided to use some of his savings and look for a place of his own. He thanked Wei for his generosity by inviting him to dim sum at a local restaurant where the two friends drank a full bottle of imported California wine and ate delicious pork and beef dishes. Wei seemed pleased on two fronts: that the two had reconnected after many years, and that Yoyo would have his own place soon. The next morning Yoyo posted his resume on *51job.com* and began searching for a place nearer to the local universities.

Yoyo soon found a place to live, in a dormitory style residence conveniently located only 600 meters south of Tsinghua U. He arrived there by taxi on a warm Sunday afternoon in late September. Yoyo was still getting settled and unpacking his small suitcase when his phone rang, from a number he did not recognize. The man on the other end of the call had a methodical manner of speaking and a mature voice. He mentioned his name but Yoyo did not hear it well. If the caller had not immediately said the word

Tsinghua, Yoyo might have hung up, mistakenly thinking it was a misdialed number.

"Good evening, I am calling from Tsinghua University," said the caller, speaking slowly in Mandarin.

"I am Professor Lin, a faculty member here at Tsinghua. I would like to speak with Mr. Yan please," he continued.

"Yes sir, this is Yoyo, Yoyo Yan."

"Well we are currently seeking some help in our department, administrative duties mainly," the professor explained. "I saw your resume earlier today and I noted that you are fluent in English."

"Yes I am," confirmed Yoyo.

"Well we are hosting a conference here in 6 weeks, so our need is quite urgent. I would like to speak with you about this position. It has been difficult to find the right person, one who has the right language skill set. Some project management skills and some translation work from Mandarin to English are required for this role."

"Well yes, that sounds very much like a job I could do, Professor," Yoyo said excitedly. "I could meet with you sometime this week. In fact, I just today moved very close to the campus, on Zhichun Road."

"Oh, I see. Where did you move here from Mr. Yan? Are you not from Beijing?"

"Well I spent the last two years as a teacher, an ESL teacher in Tibet. But I am so excited to begin living my life here in the capital."

"It appears you are living in a convenient spot.....convenient for working at the university." Lin replied.

"Oh yes, that was my intention sir. Could I meet you at your office for a discussion about this job, this great opportunity?" Yo asked hopefully, and rather boldly.

"Ahhh, well no, that's not what I am thinking," responded Mr. Lin, who then paused.

Yoyo, momentarily disappointed, remained silent since he could think of nothing persuasive to say.

Fortunately, the professor continued.....

"If you are currently on Zhichun, let's meet outside my building right now! I want to learn more about your background. You can meet me outside building #125. How does that sound to you Mr. Yan?"

Yoyo was shocked at the professor's haste, given that he had just arrived there a few hours earlier and that it was a Sunday evening. Nonetheless, Yoyo put on his only clean, white-collared shirt and his black loafers, tossed a navy blue bomber style jacket over his shoulder and walked across the street and less than 100 meters to his right. He did as he was asked; he waited on the walkway outside the professor's building. After about five minutes a short, somewhat disheveled man in his 40s emerged and introduced himself as Professor Lin. He was dressed in old tan pants that were not properly tailored for length, and a red and gold sweater that only a man without regard for fashion would purchase.

The nondescript professor suggested that they move to a nearby park for comfort and privacy while they talked about the job. Yoyo hesitated, mulling over that unusual idea. He had never heard of anyone being interviewed for a job in a public park before. He thought about asking him to verify his identity for safety, but decided against it for fear of insulting the somewhat eccentric stranger. Once again, Yo decided to take a leap of faith - maybe this man was actually a Professor in search of an employee and nothing more.

Professor Lin proved to be authentic. Indeed he was searching for an administrative assistant in the Automation Engineering department at Tsinghua. He and Yoyo discussed his needs, and the job responsibilities. The professor explained the position and asked Yoyo most questions in Mandarin, but he mixed in a few poorly worded questions in his best English, which Yoyo quickly ascertained wasn't very good. Yoyo responded in English to those inquiries, but although the older man nodded his head continuously, Yo was not sure that Lin understood some of his thoughts. Regardless, after less than an hour together meandering around the park, Lin asked Yoyo how soon he could start working with him. Yoyo could not believe his good fortune. A job offer at the iconic Tsinghua University the same day he moved out on his own in Beijing! Evidently, working for Lin seemed much better than looking for other opportunities, so he told Lin he was available right away. That brought a warm smile to the professor's face followed by a spontaneous offer:

"Well then Mr. Yan, you can start working tomorrow," was his response.

"Arrive at building 12 just before noon so I will have enough time to get your space ready, and I can find the required personnel documents. If you are in need of directions tomorrow morning, here is my contact information."

Hold on Tight

Yoyo arrived at campus, at the Second Gate just before 10:30 the next morning. Yoyo chose to arrive so early because he wanted to have time to wander the grounds and soak up the atmosphere, the ambience. Second Gate is a very impressive, prominent entrance of Roman architecture. It is a massive triple-arched white stone monument fronted by four columns reminiscent of the Pantheon. One centered, 50-foot-high arch invites people to pass through it, while two arches about half its size frame it on the sides. They also allow pedestrian traffic to pass. What he found after he went through the Gate exceeded his imagination. Tsinghua was a sprawling, beautifully landscaped campus with some classic brick buildings and some newer architecture featuring copious amounts of glass and forged steel.

Yoyo arrived at his new workplace on time, after finding the Automation Engineering building with the help of two undergraduates who noticed he looked disoriented. His first day was exciting but turned out to be uneventful. He did discover that the next six weeks of his life were likely going to require long hours, since the professor was preparing to host a conference of 25 colleagues from all over China. His workspace was adequately equipped and Yoyo spent the afternoon looking over some of the software that Lin used, occasionally asking his new boss a few questions about the conference in Mandarin. Oddly, it wasn't until that evening when he gathered his thoughts while walking home that he realized he had not even asked his new boss what he would be paid for his services. He wondered if that important detail might be found inside the legal sized envelope that was labelled "Welcome to Tsinghua" that was now in his possession.

Yoyo worked as Lin's Administrative Assistant for almost a full year. During that time he organized the details of the conference for (and served as host for) the attending guests, translated a few English studies and articles for Lin, and did final edits on some of his bosses' work, in both languages. Unfortunately, he found the subject matter on Automation Engineering quite boring, and the work itself was only rarely rewarding. What Yoyo *did* enjoy was engaging in campus life after work and on his days off. In fact, he was in some ways pretending to live the life of a student, attending many events with the undergraduates a few years his junior. He loved being on campus, so he kept a close eye on the dignitaries and various guest speakers who were scheduled to come to the university. He attended at least one event per month that year. Additionally, he spent almost all of his free time on weekends at the Tsinghua recreation hub; as a staff member it was available to him for swimming, jogging on the indoor track, and playing badminton.

Living on his own, Yoyo missed his family - his mother's stern commands and special recipes, his father's occasional smiles, his sister's laugh and empathetic ear. He thought about that call his father made a few weeks earlier, prior to his employment. He decided he would follow through and invite his father to see the big city that Dad had such reverence for, Yoyo's new home. He knew the visit would have to be after the conference ended, and Beijing is more enjoyable in the springtime anyway. Yoyo and his dad decided that the last week in March would be the best time for his vacation. The young son purchased a train ticket for his father and arranged a downtown hotel for them both to stay in.

During their time together father and son visited Tiananmen Square and the massive Memorial Hall, also known as the Mausoleum of Mao. It houses the embalmed/mummified body of Mao Zedong, who is to this day laying in a crystal coffin. Mao Zedong was the Chairman/ leader of the Communist Party for 33 years, right up until the time of his death in 1976. Built in 1977, right after Chairman Mao's death, the exterior of the Hall features 44 impressive granite columns standing on the large burgundy granite base which supports the golden roof. While touring the resting place of one of Dad's idols, his father's awe for the departed leader made him misty eyed. He was clearly overcome with emotion, and he said something very loving, and therefore very memorable for Yoyo: *"Long Live Zhonghua".* Yoyo often thought about why his father said such beautiful words to him on that lovely spring day. That moment, and the rest of his visit to Beijing, would prove to repair much of the damage done to their relationship in earlier years. In fact, only four months later, in August, the Yan clan would once again choose to live together, but this time in Beijing.

Gay friendly websites and online chat rooms were starting to become more popular in 2005, and Yoyo started to become more aware of them during his time in Beijing. Before and after his father's visit occurred, Yoyo used the internet to dip his toe into the sea of gay life. He chatted with dozens of men, using the anonymity of the internet to give him more courage. After meeting up with a half dozen guys for drinks and dialogue, he finally found a man he connected with. Having just turned 40, he was almost 15 years older than Yoyo. Jun had a really good job, working as a trainer for the biggest auto company in China. He dressed professionally, and Yoyo loved his style, his colourful and extensive wardrobe.

After seeing each other a few times at tea houses and restaurants, they were finding it quite difficult to control their mutual attraction. They had found enough privacy in the park to kiss and do some touching a couple of times, but nothing more. Jun had a high libido, and was making his interest in having sex with his younger companion more and more apparent with each date. Yoyo felt the same way, although the means and methods of gay sex were still largely a mystery to him. Unfortunately, Yo could not host people at his dormitory style residence. They knew they would have to look elsewhere for the privacy they were seeking.

One Saturday morning in the early summer of 2005, Jun surprised Yoyo by calling him with some exciting news; which was potentially the opportunity they were looking for. If Yoyo could get time off work, Jun would be able to take him on his work trip to Changchun. They would go by train, an overnight trip with a sleeper car. They would have to depart on a Wednesday and arrive on Thursday morning. From there they would spend two nights in Changchun in a company sponsored hotel room, then depart for home on Saturday. As a man who was always up for adventure and new experiences, Yoyo agreed to consider going with his beguiling new boyfriend.

Earlier that week, Yoyo had been in contact with Cisco Systems, the Fortune 500 Company based in California. Cisco's Beijing office needed to hire a handful of English interpreters to liaise between the US executives and their Chinese affiliate colleagues. His second interview was scheduled for the following Tuesday morning, three days after Jun's offer. He told Jun that he wanted to go on the trip with him, but since he was thinking about switching jobs, the timing of the offer wasn't very good. Furthermore, Yoyo had never asked Professor Lin for any vacation days, so he was uncertain how amenable his boss would be if he did so now. Jun seemed to understand all of that, and simply told him that it was an open offer, and he was still hopeful Yoyo could make himself available.

The next interview with Cisco went quite well. Yoyo felt that they were very close to offering him the job, and the HR person at Cisco said a decision would be made by the end of that week. Yoyo called Jun on Tuesday evening and told him that he had a plan; a plan that quite likely meant they would be able to travel to Changchun together. He would ask Professor Lin if he could have a vacation week before the next academic year began in September. If it was approved, he would then inform Lin that the week he wanted was aligned with Jun's work trip to northwest China. But if the professor put up any barriers, Yoyo told Jun that he planned to quit working for him if and when the Cisco job offer came through as expected. He could tell Cisco that he was available to start his new position the Monday after they returned. He explained with gusto that either way, he was planning on joining him. He slipped in a reference to wanting safe sex, and tacitly mentioned that he would bring what they needed.

Yoyo waited until the following week to approach Professor Lin with his time off request, after Cisco had offered him the translation job. The leverage of having that opportunity emboldered Yoyo, and although he did not really want to leave the campus life, he felt it was time to make some real money. He wanted to leave the dorm life, and find a nice apartment where he could entertain Jun and his other friends. The Cisco offer was almost double the annual pay than he was earning at Tsinghua - he would be earning 100,000 yuan if he accepted.

Professor Lin, never having had an assistant before, seemed taken aback by Yoyo's request. He asked Yo if he expected the week off to be paid or unpaid. Yoyo replied that he wanted the former, and also asked his boss if his pay would increase after he had been with him for a full year. Lin said he would look into the request for paid time off, but he gave no indication that any pay escalation was forthcoming. He pushed the discussion further by politely asking if Yoyo was looking for other opportunities at the university, leaving Lin. Yoyo deftly changed the subject without giving him an answer. He had options, but the status quo did not seem like the best one.

After more than nine months working at Tsinghua, Yoyo Yan became a former employee on July 8, 2005. He accepted the Cisco offer, and told them he could start working for them any time after Sunday, July 24th. Not coincidentally, Jun's work trip was scheduled for July 20th to July 23rd.

Years of confusion, avoidance, shame, repressed sexual urges, and enjoyment of the sly romantic sessions with Aki were on his mind as he and Jun boarded their overnight train. Yoyo was excited, anticipating that his first time would be with an older, experienced lover that he really respected and cared for. He came well prepared. He had purchased some 2xist branded underwear, a tight fitting black t-shirt and a bottle of wine for their excursion.

The two of them found the dark ambiance of the overnight train to be romantic, and flirted with one another until it was time to find the sleeper car. They were able to have some cuddle time as they crammed themselves into one single bunk; but the main event would have to wait. There were far too many other people nearby. The overhead speaker woke them from their dozing just after 6:00 a.m., with the announcement from the conductor that their arrival time would be in 30 minutes.

They arrived at their hotel and found it very much to their liking. Their time in Changchun would be short, but Jun had a surprise in mind to maximize their time together. While he led his training sessions, he wanted to take Yoyo with him. Jun told Yoyo he would be introducing him as his assistant trainer, with a phony name....Phoenix Yang. Yoyo laughed, and said he thought that was a bad idea but he had nothing else to do, so yes, he would go along for the ride. The pair returned to the hotel after the dinner hour, but food was not their main priority - feasting on their carnal desires was.

Once they were safely behind the locked door, they embraced and kissed like they were passengers on the Titanic. Yoyo, always courteous and cognizant of hygiene, took a pause and announced that he wanted to shower before they did anything physical. Jun agreed and gave Yo a gentle kiss before they separated momentarily.

Jun was a "top", just as Yoyo had hoped. Yo's instincts led him to believe that he would enjoy being with a more dominant man. Jun approached his younger lover and began delivering butterfly kisses on the nape of his neck. He then descended slowly while working his way down Yoyo's back. That feeling was the moment of no return for his sexuality, at least physically. After that sizzling appetizer Yoyo was anticipating the entrée. He smiled nervously, and invited his lover to climb aboard.

Chapter 11 *Better Together*

J un took his wife and young daughter to see the red maple leaves of Xiangshan a few weeks later. Yoyo was not invited. He was able to get Jun's attention a few times that autumn, but the romance fizzled. Married, bisexual men tend to be less than reliable lovers - a lesson Yoyo, and many others after him, had to learn the hard way. By December of that year, it was clear to Yoyo that Jun was not the one for him, despite the strong affection he felt. Very reluctantly, after numerous emails and texts went unanswered, Yoyo knew he had to move on from the man who took his virginity, but the one who validated his sexual identity.

While working for Cisco as he was recovering from Jun's heartbreak, Yoyo became extremely lonely. He called home with an idea. For the first time in his life, he was in a financial position to help his parents. Yoyo invited his parents (and subsequently a very pregnant Meiying and her husband) to live with him in the capital. He wanted to be present for the birth of his nephew. He sent them a detailed description of a relatively spacious three bedroom apartment he had just rented in the Xuanwu district. It was a big ask, but the offer came at the right time. Yo's parents were struggling to find reliable help and did not have the requisite energy to run the business by themselves anymore. Additionally, Meiying and her husband had been thinking of moving from Wenzhou to Beijing to find better employment opportunities. He was pleased that only four days later his parents boarded an overnight coach train heading north. Clearly they were eager to reunite with their only son.

The Yan family reunion became complete when sister Meiying and her husband arrived four weeks later in early April of 2007, more than nine years after Yoyo left home. The furnished apartment was an eye-popping upgrade for Yoyo's parents, who had both celebrated their 52nd birthdays recently. They were not accustomed to having essentials like fully stocked grocers and plentiful hot water; not to mention new luxuries like cable television and a desktop computer connected to the internet. Meiying seemed particularly pleased to be in Beijing, where she was closer to excellent doctors and hospitals for her last trimester. Yoyo's dad found work doing maintenance in an office building only three subway stops from their new home. He was not a man who liked to have a lot of idle time, so he too was pleased with the decision to relocate to the capital.

Baby Shen Shen arrived on July 13th. He was like a gift from the heavens - for so many reasons. China's controversial One Child Policy did slow population growth, but it also had the unintended effect of making every child even more precious for the entire extended family. Shen's parents and his two grandparents were absolutely thrilled to have a healthy boy to dote on. He was constantly being smothered with attention and love. Additionally, in this case, his birth was also like a pressure relief valve for Yoyo. Sons are expected to find a wife in their 20s, and start a family soon thereafter. Well, the straight ones are anyway. Shen Shen's arrival was a joyous distraction to his parents....and it bought Yo more time to work on his career and his love life. Fortunately, it created a temporary ceasefire of the probing questions regarding his relationship status. Yoyo had accepted his own sexuality, but was still hiding deep in the closet for his family.

Yoyo always had a close-knit relationship with his sister, going back to the days when they walked to school together and repelled the bullies. This period together strengthened that sibling bond. In fact, he trusted Meiying wholeheartedly. Consequently, Yo decided he wanted to share his sexuality with her, coming out of the closet, albeit only for a peek outside. Unfortunately, for LGBTQ individuals sharing their secret is a daunting and often confounding task. That fear is magnified in a country like China, where most people born before the 1980s cannot even fathom the concept of their child being homosexual.

Yoyo finally found his voice, and the opportunity to tell Meiying privately and without distractions one afternoon while his parents were out shopping. How exactly to phrase the revelation is something many queer people mull over/rehearse quite carefully. Yo prefaced their chat by informing her that their conversation was of a very personal nature, and even admitted that he was nervous about it. He plodded on, saying a string of words that he had never said aloud:

> "My sister, you are the only person in the world that knows what I am going to tell you. I trust you and want to share my truth with you.....*big pause and a deep breath*......I am attracted to men."

A heavy silence ensued for what seemed like minutes as Meiying processed this news. She nodded but did not give away her feeling with any facial expression, and before she could reply Yoyo blurted out an unscripted but entirely unnecessary sentence.....

> "Please do not tell mom or dad!"

Meiying ended her silence, with a comforting smile and some words Yoyo needed to hear...

"Don't worry. This is a secret I will not tell anyone Yoyo. This kind of relationship can be very hard - but I will support your choices however I can."

Meiying then asked only two clarifying questions....

"Do you have a boyfriend now?" and "How do you know this is true if you have never had a girlfriend?"

The two of them discussed the situation for only a few minutes before changing the subject, but those few minutes and Meiying's warm and caring demeanour is something Yoyo still remembers fondly.

Without privacy for romance in the apartment, Yoyo spent the rest of 2007 focusing his energy on being a caring uncle and on his work at Cisco. Although he occasionally checked social media for uniformed men he thought might be gay, he was able to put his desire for romance aside at that point. He was learning what life was like as a family man. His bond with his nephew was so strong that his sister often said that Yoyo was a third parent to Shen Shen. There was no time for the chase or for the catch, so a new boyfriend would have to wait.

While life at home was joyful, the job at Cisco was not going well. Yoyo found the content of the work uninspiring, and although the corporate culture seemed supportive enough, he was not enjoying any of it. His love of analysis, storytelling, and reporting was not a good fit for work at a technology company. He became the kind of employee who was only working for the money, never arriving early or staying late. He was only mildly surprised that he got fired at his one year performance review.

Self-awareness and determination are the twin towers of career development, and fortunately Yoyo Yan was blessed with both. With three other family members earning incomes, he realized that he had the opportunity to take his time and find the right job. After only a few days of contemplation, and for the first time since attaining his English degree, Yo decided that he wanted to try working as a journalist. He spent a couple of months at home looking at job boards and bonding with Shen Shen. As an uncle, those months were extremely transformative. For the first time in his life, Yoyo absolutely knew he wanted his own children.

Notice of a job fair landed in his inbox one afternoon late in 2007. Yoyo found a large news agency booth adorned in traditional red and gold decor. Xinhua is by far the largest news agency in China, and has correspondents in more than 150 countries. Yoyo knew that the ubiquitous Xinhua agency also published newspapers and magazines in several languages, including English. He thought that such an expansive organization must have some vacancies for bilingual staff. Yoyo spoke briefly with the representative and left his resume for their consideration.

Several days later he took a call from the agency's HR department. They wanted to assess his English proficiency before starting the formal interviewing process. He was summoned to one of the bureaus nearest to him for a written test, which he passed easily. Ten days later he was back at the bureau and found himself in much deeper waters. On this round of screening, he was asked to join four other well educated candidates for formal interviewing in a group setting. Facing that kind of pressure was a first for the young man from Jiangxi province. As if that wasn't scary enough, early on in the group/panel interview Yoyo discovered the size of the sharks he was swimming with.

The other candidates were all educated in the USA or in British postgraduate programs. One of them even held a Ph.D. in sinology (the study of Chinese language, history, customs, and politics). Despite being the one candidate who held only a domestic bachelor's degree, Yoyo clearly impressed the panel of newsmen. He was offered the position. Although he was a bit disappointed with the salary offered, he quickly accepted. Yo had his eye on a much larger prize. He correctly anticipated that Xinhua could jumpstart his career and likely proffer him an overseas opportunity, ideally a country with better gay rights and more available men.

His main responsibility at his new job was doing copyediting for English news reporters. He would scan their stories carefully and provide ideas for improvement before press deadlines. Yoyo loved the pace of the work, and totally devoted himself to this new career path. His bosses were impressed with his work and they eventually provided him with more appropriate compensation.

In 2008, the upcoming summer Olympics became a massive story in China. Although the Beijing Games were not scheduled to begin until the second week of August, the preceding months were a magical time; it was an especially exciting time to be a journalist there. This was the first time China was chosen to host the Olympics, and the Communist Party really wanted to disseminate a message of unity and desperately wanted to promote their emerging economy to the international audience. This created a wide array of story lines and an opportunity for a state controlled news agency like Xinhua to be a good soldier....marching to the drumbeat emanating from President Hu.

In the summer of that year, 204 countries sent just shy of 11,000 athletes to compete at the Olympic Games. The opening ceremony was a massive, multi-dimensional spectacle that Yoyo had the privilege of covering from a very high perch in the gondola at the top of the "Birds Nest", the newly built Olympic Stadium. Widely considered to be the best ever opening ceremonies, the Chinese Party spent over $100 million on the event. They even used the nascent weather modification techniques available at that time to control the weather by preventing rain that evening.

The leaders of the People's Republic of China faced widespread criticism as they prepared for the 2008 Olympics. Western media was accusing China of human rights violations and poor treatment of Tibetan dissidents. The air quality in and around Beijing was perceived to be too hazardous to the lungs of so many high performance athletes. In response, the Communist Party regime agreed to reduce CO_2 emissions by closing factories a few months ahead of time, and also by restrictions on traffic (only allowing citizens to drive vehicles on certain days to reduce polluting auto emissions).

Yoyo was blessed, yet sometimes burdened, with a honey badger temperament. Consequently, as 2008 came to a close he was restless; he was looking for an opportunity to leave China to seek independence, more adventure, and a muscular man to love. The closing ceremonies were eventful, exhilarating, and emotional. Despite that, paradoxically, Yoyo left the stadium that night with an odd feeling of personal angst....an event that was so important for so many other Chinese actually made Yoyo more eager to leave the country. Later on, he realized that the Games were actually a bittersweet farewell to the life and culture he had known for 27 years.

Chapter 12 *Istanbul or Islamabad?*

S hortly after the Olympics, Yoyo started to pursue a foreign assignment by signing up for Xinhua's annual "expatriate selection" exams. One day in the spring of 2009 the HR department at the agency called Yoyo and said they had an opportunity to send a reporter to their Islamabad bureau; which he incorrectly identified as the biggest city in **Turkey.** Only the next day would he realize he was not heading to the relatively quiet Istanbul, rather he would be sent to a geopolitical hotspot, a war zone. He returned to the apartment that night knowing he would have to have a long discussion with his parents about his career, and he would ask for their approval before making such a life-altering move. He thought about finally coming out to them, to fully explain why he wanted to be "freer", by leaving China. Once again, he decided to wait.

In the wee hours of May 2nd 2011, United States Navy Seal Team Six successfully conducted their mission to find and capture or kill Al-Qaeda's leader, Osama Bin Laden, in Abbottabad, Pakistan. Under the cover of darkness, 25 well trained Navy Seals risked their lives after years of planning and reams of intelligence collection. The entire death defying operation was over only 40 minutes after the two choppers arrived. Their target was located and shot to death in only nine minutes. According to the US Military, Bin-Laden's body was quickly taken out of the secret compound and buried at sea less than 24 hours later, in accordance with Islamic customs, ostensibly to prevent his grave from becoming a shrine for his followers.

Abbottabad is not far from Xinhua's Pakistani bureau in Islamabad, where young Yoyo was working. He and several other Asian reporters received the news of the raid early that Monday morning and knew they needed to get to the site immediately. Fueled by an adrenaline rush and the desire to cover this huge story regardless of the obvious risks, the team of Xinhua reporters rousted their reliable driver and left the bureau just before 9:00 a.m. As they approached Abbottabad in their unmarked grey Toyota sedan, the three journalists discussed various ways they could cover the story. Suddenly, while cruising along the N35 Expressway and only about six miles from their destination, a deafening sound unlike any the men had heard before shook their vehicle; causing Tariq the driver to momentarily swerve off the paved road. While the reporters did not realize it at that time, loyal Al-Qaeda supporters were white hot angry and had begun firing RPG-7 bombs at selected roadways leading to the Bin Laden compound. That particular shoulder fired RPG missile landed in a spot the reporters had driven over less than 10 seconds earlier. Fortunately, a startled Tariq regained control of the vehicle as he repeatedly shouted "allah yufiquna"(*God help us)* in Arabic. He gathered himself, and then sped up as they drove on in shocked silence as they waited for the ringing in their ears to subside.

When they reached the site of the raid, nerves frayed from their brush with disaster, the journalists found organized chaos. There were dozens of press, local residents, and armed police clustered together. It appeared to Yoyo that the barricade they encountered was quite a distance, about 300 meters from the compound and the smoldering UH60 Blackhawk helicopter that the Seals had left behind. After exiting their vehicle, they relied on Yoyo's strong English skills and his loyal companion Zeeshan's knowledge of Pashto to gather as much information as they could. What they discovered was that the Pakistani police had set up an impromptu checkpoint to screen the press corps - with the intention of allowing only journalists without cameras to pass and walk closer to the scene. Their mandate was to ensure that no photos near the scene would be permitted.

After almost an hour of wandering around outside the checkpoint, gathering bits and pieces of unverified information, the Xinhua crew's frustration was palpable. Yoyo wanted to smuggle his camera inside the forbidden zone, but how? He devised a dubious plan. Before they left the office, he had heard Tariq mention his day off and the joy of playing with his two young children. Yo wondered if maybe he still had the family baby stroller stored in the trunk of the company Toyota. He made the inquiry but was disappointed with the answer. Shortly thereafter, while the journalists were still outside the area mulling over their options, Yoyo's eagle eye spotted a couple walking on an adjacent street walking away from the chaos, pushing what appeared to be a baby stroller. He hastily asked his colleagues how much US cash they were carrying. After some puzzled looks and several questions he had no time to answer, he got the crew to empty their pockets. Including his own money he had access to $325.

Yoyo took the cash, grabbed his Pashto speaking friend, and said he would return. He passed his camera bag to one of his other companions and ran towards the family he had seen moments before. Yoyo certainly wasn't going to be confused with an Olympic sprinter, but he was able to chase down the slower moving couple with the baby stroller. He adjusted his pace and approached them cautiously, walking slowly as he got closer. He got their attention by yelling and waving the wad of bills, simultaneously gesturing at the stroller they were pushing. Clearly, they were both confused and afraid. He needed help to be understood, so he immediately told his friend to offer the man $300 in exchange for the stroller. Fortunately, the reporter who spoke their language rather fluently was able to make them understand that the reporters did not want **their baby**, but only wanted their shabby looking baby conveyance. $300US was more than the average labourer takes home in a month in Islamabad, so the deal was made.

The optics of two young Chinese men pushing a baby stroller down a street in an Islamic country like Pakistan was, even for a gay man, unseemly. Yoyo collapsed the stroller and carried it over his shoulder as they hustled back to where the action was. Now that the journalists had their expensive, albeit wobbly stroller, the question on everyone but Yoyo's minds was "what the heck are we going to do with it?" Using an emergency blanket that was stored in the trunk of the driver's car, they were able to wrap their camera equipment up, with the objective of making it resemble the shape of a toddler sitting in the baby seat.

Incredibly, due to the chaos on the ground and possibly his cherubic appearance, Yoyo was able to pass discreetly through the checkpoint pushing the stroller and their cameras. His colleagues showed their press credentials and breezed through as well, after minimal questioning. Unfortunately, when they got as close as security forces would allow them to, the three reporters realized there was not much to see. The Bin Laden compound was constructed only a few years earlier with privacy in mind, so it had 18 foot concrete walls topped with barbed wire. Fortunately, Yoyo was able to get a few photos of several pieces of the disabled US Blackhawk chopper, since part of the remains fell on the exterior of the compound when it crashed.

The report Yoyo filed that evening was one of several he would write that week, as details of how the American forces pulled off the surprise raid surfaced. Here is an excerpt from

Yan's story, the report that was published by the agency in the China Daily News on May 3:

*"Unconfirmed reports here in Islamabad say that there were a total of five casualties in the Abbottabad ambush: Osama Bin Laden, his son Khalid, and three other as yet unnamed people who appear to have been living with Bin Laden in the compound. No Americans were killed or injured. Sources from the US State Department have not weighed in on the record, but my sources tell me it seems that the US did not have permission from the Pakistani government to conduct this mission inside their borders. Apparently, Obama was not 100% certain this was the safe house where Osama Bin Laden was hiding, but he went ahead and authorized the raid anyway. **Osama Bin Laden seemed have been buried in the sea of questions.** Three of the most salient questions that still need to be answered in the days ahead are…. Absent any photos of the corpse and without any other clear evidence, how can anyone be sure the Americans are telling the truth about killing him? If it was indeed Bin Laden's hideout, did the Pakistani Intelligence Service (government) aid and abet Bin Laden living there? And if they did how will harboring a terrorist of his stature affect Pakistan's relationship with the US and the world community?"*

Another memorable event during his time working in Pakistan was when Yoyo was embedded with nine other international journalists, who were allowed to travel on an American Chinook helicopter that was taking humanitarian aid to a flooded area in Swat Valley. The press were invited along and encouraged to shoot lots of pictures - it was part of a US forces image building mission to generate positive publicity. In the words of Secretary of State Hilary Clinton, defeating and driving out the Taliban was most effectively accomplished by winning the hearts and minds of the Pakistani people. Regardless of what one thinks about American foreign policy and often dubious decision making post 9-11, there is no doubt that this war on terror was a unique career development opportunity for the young journalist from rural China.

In retrospect, covering Bin Laden's assassination and embedding with US humanitarian missions, combined with an opportunity to participate in scrum interviews with Clinton and Angelina Jolie, were the highlights of his Pakistan assignment. However, many other days were not nearly as exhilarating. It takes a very strong will to endure more than two years of daily pressures and intermittent anguish that derives from reporting on the continuous conflicts between Taliban militants and NATO-led security forces; not to mention waking up every day realizing you are living in one of the most volatile and violent global hotspots. Yoyo was also dealing with two extremely demanding bureau chiefs at various points in his tenure in Islamabad. His circumstances certainly forced him to grow up quickly, ultimately forging fine lines on his face and even harder lines in his mind. While Yoyo Yan may not have been a NATO soldier, he still emerged as a bit of a warrior.

Chapter 13

The Land of the Brave, the Graveyard of Empires

W **elcome to the land of the brave.** Those were the words Yoyo saw on the massive rectangular greeting sign at the Kabul international airport. Apparently his Xinhua bosses had been impressed with his work in Pakistan, so in late 2011 they decided to send their rising star to Afghanistan with a new title: Bureau Chief. That was the good news. The bad news was that Afghanistan was in total disarray. Even compared to Pakistan, Afghanistan was far more ravaged by conflict, violent wars and human suffering. Disputes about the government of the day, religious beliefs, and the merits of the Taliban were routinely settled with dastardly acts of hatred and destruction. The Afghan people had been living in turmoil and without a functioning economy for decades. It was a very depressing situation. Fortunately, Yoyo was young and resolute, so he was up for the adventure.

If you are 40 years old or younger and still alive in Afghanistan, your entire life has been lived in a war zone, with only brief periods of relative calm. Since the Russian invasion of 1979, conflict and danger for Afghans has been the one constant. Civil wars between various governing bodies and the Mujahedeen (jihadists) were complete quagmires, destabilizing the economy and killing or injuring over 1.5 million men, women, and children. Additionally, rough estimates are that two million Afghan people are refugees and/or displaced from their homes due to the ceaseless fighting. All of that suffering happening in a country with a population smaller than Canada's. The human costs are staggering.

The Afghan economy is not well capitalized and is therefore almost entirely agrarian. Farming (mainly fruits, nuts, and opium) and wool products make up almost all of the production output. Only about $1 billion worth of goods are exported annually to two main trading partners, India and Pakistan. Economic freedom is ranked around 135th of 200 countries indexed. In fact, Yoyo felt as if he had been sent backwards in a time machine, moving from a surging China, then on to Pakistan, and finally to one of the poorest countries in the world - the Islamic Emirate of Afghanistan.

Despite all of the poverty and the danger surrounding them, Yoyo and his press colleagues found regular Afghan people to be honest, reliable, and almost always friendly to foreigners. As Bureau Chief, Yo had to hire support staff for the Kabul office where the seven reporters worked and lived. They were supported by two armed guards, two drivers, and a housekeeper/cook named Didi. Like so many Afghan women in her generation, Didi was a widow - her husband had been killed 10 years earlier by the Taliban. She always wore a taupe or lavender coloured hijab which covered her long hair and neck, but left her smooth tan cheeks and warm hazel eyes exposed. Her marital 'status' meant she faced an even greater personal security threat, since widowed women were prohibited from working outside the home by Islamic fundamentalist law. A few of Didi's male neighbours and others who knew her situation would occasionally verbally and even physically assault her when she had the audacity to simply walk alone in the streets outside her home. Despite this constant oppression, Didi was resolute. She ignored the taunts and harassment and worked at the Chinese news bureau because she had three children to feed and care for.

Didi was a daily visitor to the Xinhua news office. She did the laundry and prepared lunch so the reporters could increase their productivity. The journalists were particularly fond of Didi's lamb rib and rice dish. Yo also truly enjoyed her presence due to her perpetually upbeat personality. In time Yoyo came to realize that Didi was not a unicorn, rather she was symbolic of the resilience and spirit of the Afghan people. It became evident that she was not the only one blessed with those traits.

For the past several years, Yoyo had been focusing on this new career and mostly ignoring his libido. Obviously, reporting in war zones is not exactly an aphrodisiac. However, for the first time since it ended badly with Jun, Yoyo was able to find a lover. One of Yoyo's ongoing fantasies was being wooed by and making love with a sophisticated European man. He would often think about the accents and physical features of Italian or Spanish men, but one of his most recurring fantasies during his university years was to meet and fall in love with a Frenchman. Luckily for the both of them, a few months after getting settled in Kabul, he met a French national who was there on assignment as well. Kabul was anything but Paris, but when Yoyo was with Stefan the chaos of conflict came to a halt, and he almost couldn't tell the difference.

Stefan was working for an international aid NGO called Action Contre la Faim France. On this mission, he had been there only a few months longer than Yoyo, but was on his third tour of duty in Afghanistan. At 185 cm, he was the tallest man Yoyo had ever been with. He was also the oldest. His dark brown hair was graying slightly on the sides at the temple. Stefan referred to it using a term Yo had never heard before - salt and pepper. It was often tousled and slightly out of control; indicating Stefan had priorities other than fastidious personal grooming. In his youth he had been a competitive athlete, even winning the BTC tennis tournament when he was age 29. Twenty years later, his muscular physique was now carrying extra abdominal weight - which Yoyo usually finds attractive. Additionally, Stefan had a unique temperament. Yoyo loved that he was athletic, and liked Stefan's ability to tell entertaining tales of his past trips and shenanigans with family and friends. Stefan had not been to China before, but he had traveled extensively for pleasure in Europe and as an aid worker in South America. Like Yoyo, Stefan earned his education through a mix of academic reading, travel, and life experiences. They seemed to be a perfect match.

For their rendezvous Yoyo met up with Stefan by getting his driver Abdul to drop him off at his lover's sparsely furnished NGO rental house. Their relationship started out with sporadic, brief encounters, but after their fifth date they became regular lovers with overnight visits as the norm. For several months Yoyo made time for Stefan once a week regardless of his deadlines and other commitments as Bureau Chief. Not since he spent time with Mr. Tutu had Yoyo felt such a connection and riveting vibe with a man. The sex was fun and passionate, to the point where Yoyo fondly recalls that it was common for items adjacent to the bed to get knocked off their perches. While dating Stefan, Yoyo had a lot to learn about intimacy, and his new lover was very happy to be his sexual mentor. Thus, it was a time of experimentation and amazing new experiences. The two lovers enjoyed cuddling in the afterglow, occasionally joking that some yoga classes don't require that much flexibility.

A more unlikely but nonetheless special friendship Yoyo created during this period was with one of the drivers mentioned above: Abdul Qadir. When Yoyo felt homesick or under the influence of extreme stressors, Abdul would occasionally offer to drive the "chief" up to the top of the mountain, for some quiet time. Yoyo would take his music player up with him and let his mind wander to various places, especially his homeland. One of those occasions was the day after a shockingly close encounter with death, even closer than the RPG missile that almost got him 14 months earlier.

One afternoon in June of 2012 the reporters were working on a story about President Obama's recently announced timetable for the steady and imminent withdrawal of US forces and a proposed handover to Afghan military success. Suddenly, their world was rocked by a jarring bomb blast. The Xinhua Kabul bureau office/residence was located in Wazir Akbar Khan district, known locally as the diplomatic zone, just steps away from the Norwegian Embassy. On that day, the Taliban's target was actually a nearby Lebanese restaurant, which was known to be popular with western diplomats and foreign journalists. There were 14 fatalities, and almost 100 people were injured to various degrees on that day. At the bureau, their close proximity resulted in shattered glass and a damaged exterior wall.

Upon hearing the blast Yoyo and his colleagues scrambled to relocate themselves to a basement safe house to continue covering the developing terror attack that they were suddenly immersed in. Throughout the harrowing evening and well into the wee hours of the morning the journalist crew were busy, swiftly filing stories to Beijing, to Hong Kong, and to the New York editorial departments. It was a stressful and very eventful night, interspersed with regular communication to the local Chinese embassy to ascertain the impact on and monitor for casualties in the Chinese community. The reporters were on edge fearing another blast. Despite their trepidation, they bravely searched for and interviewed several witnesses.

In the weeks that followed it was up to Yoyo to arrange and oversee implementation of increased security measures like a new steel gate and two layers of two meter high sandbags piled high along the exterior walls. Although those was difficult days, he was undeterred.

Nearing the end of his time in Kabul and on a relatively peaceful day under blue sky and sunshine, Abdul drove Yoyo all the way up to Northern Afghanistan, a very scenic region of the war-torn paradise known as the Panjshir. Yoyo wanted to spend a day paying a tribute to the memorial site for the "Lion of Panjshir", General Ahmad Shah Massoud. Massoud is the revered military leader of the Northern Alliance who first fought off the invading Soviet forces beginning in 1979, and who then later commanded thousands of soldiers that successfully kept his home province free of the Taliban's fundamental interpretation of Islam. The date of his death, September 9th, is a national holiday in Afghanistan known as Massoud Day.

Yoyo was captivated by the Legend of the Lion....the Afghan commander/hero that his chauffeur Abdul had fought with and talked so much about. Prior to his trip Yoyo studied some of the inspiring details of the General's biography. Despite allocating far more men, tanks and other weaponry on six different attempts taking their land in the early '80s, the Soviets were unable to defeat Massoud's Afghan forces. The Soviet commanders became increasingly frustrated with the resistance, so by 1982 the Soviets began deploying major combat units in the Panjshir, with estimates of 30,000 men in that region alone. Amazingly, Massoud was savvy enough to outmaneuver the Soviet invaders by repositioning his troops in hideaway valleys, where they occupied strategic positions which allowed his fighters many successful ambushes. Eventually the weary Soviets withdrew, but not before over 2,500 of them were captured and interrogated by Massoud's makeshift army.

Hold on Tight

During his brief journey up to the Panjshir valley, Yoyo was pleased to find very helpful people and a breathtaking topography of mountains, deep, lush valleys and winding rivers. In the old villages and towns he visited, a sharp contrast existed. There was little beauty to be found; rather he encountered severely damaged, windowless houses that were long ago left partially or mostly in ruins - with unattended piles of concrete and household debris strewn about. He also saw several men and one child left crippled after they lost a leg to a stray land mine. Surreal outdoor "museums" such as the Soviet tank field were still there, ostensibly as trophies of the Afghan victory years ago.

The territory now known as Afghanistan has achieved the rather unique distinction of being known as the "graveyard of empires". That moniker derives from the various attempted conquests dating back centuries. Just in the last 200 years three empires have not learned the lessons of history. Britain, which was the most dominant empire in the mid-1800s, learned the hard way that pacifying dozens of tribes with their own subcultures is a herculean task. In more recent times, both the Soviets and the Americans have decided to try their own unwelcome incursions into Afghanistan; burning through ridiculous amounts of resources and human lives in the process. After the Americans finally leave empty handed - and they almost assuredly will - China seems positioned to be the next emerging empire that might try to find the keys to open the doors to this geopolitical hotspot. That thought was oddly comforting to Yoyo even though he was not sure he wanted to live in China in the future.

Kevin McCaffrey

Chapter **14** *Seeking a Safer Harbour*

Y oyo spent his free time in Afghanistan reading and dreaming about countries that were blessed with better LGBTQ rights and freedoms. In April of 2013 Yoyo's time reporting news from war zones had come to its conclusion. He was entitled to a one month vacation during this transitional period after his replacement arrived to take over the bureau in Kabul. His boss initially proposed a move to Finland to lead the Helsinki bureau. Yo quickly declined; he wanted to be someplace with a larger population and more going on. He briefly considered asking to work in bustling New York City, but subsequently had second thoughts. Yo believed that in a much larger bureau like New York he would be placed into a subordinate role - he feared being a soldier asked to report on the price of corn and soybeans exports rather than continuing to be stimulated acting as a General. He decided he would bide his time in Beijing and wait for immigration approval to work as Bureau Chief in Toronto. Although he was not aware of it at the time, if Yoyo took the Toronto job he would have the distinction of being Xinhua's youngest employee ever to serve as a chief in North America.

It was easy to acquire the credentials to work in Islamabad and Kabul, but getting the visa for Canada proved to be a different animal altogether. Canadian officials had and still have significant suspicions about many Chinese journalists, rooted in a cloud of mistrust. Unfortunately for someone who loves to be busy, the temporary permit to work in the Toronto bureau took six months to acquire. He bided his time in Beijing, burdened with uncertainty about his future.

During much of that period Yoyo spent time resting and adjusting to a peaceful life. He loved playing with his nephew Shen Shen, and taught the youngster as much as he could. Additionally, as he entered his 30s as a gay man, Yoyo was simultaneously dealing with uncomfortable inquiries into his personal life and reeling from the pervasive and often explicit parental pressures of marrying and having children. Such a perception of urgency began to weigh heavily on his mind. Suddenly he had lots of free time, and consequently Yoyo was eager to find a boyfriend and a long-term relationship. He was a frequent visitor to Grindr and other gay dating websites. For a few months he became entangled in a doomed relationship with a divorced and deeply closeted father of a nine year old daughter. Any queer person knows that same-sex relationships are challenging in and of themselves, but when one partner is closeted and living fearfully about their identity, the challenges seem to amplify. The details often differ, but the end result is almost always the same. Over time the secrecy, the paranoia, and the inability to be comfortable in public places culminates in stressors that cannot be overcome.

Eventually, the international reporter was cleared by CSIS and allowed to fy to Canada. Zhonghua (Yoyo) Yan arrived at Pearson International Airport on September 30, 2013 with two suitcases and some ambitious goals. A work visa had finally been issued and he was excited about this safer harbour and learning about the west. He soon discovered that the Bureau Chief role in Toronto was everything he hoped it would be and more. He and his crew of expatriate Chinese journalists had more autonomy than ever. They used that autonomy as inspiration to pursue stories from coast to coast, visiting every province/territory except Newfoundland and Nunavut.

Yoyo and two of his colleagues quickly decided to join a touring group for an exciting excursion to Northwest Territories on the Arctic Circle - to observe and report on the culture and way of life in the far north. They spent 10 days visiting with several Inuit families and their tribal chiefs. Where else in the world would one be able to dine on whale meat while hearing incredible stories of extreme climate hardship and human ingenuity? Inuit storytelling and writing are essential for passing on cultural traditions and important values to younger community members. The touring group learned about First Nations intense reverence of nature and the Inuit's strong belief in pleasing the spirits surrounding them; and conversely the intense fear that ignoring the spirits would bring them much misery. Sedna, the Goddess of the Sea who lived on the seafloor, was considered the most powerful spirit. She was the one that could control the bounties of food supply.

Another interesting story they wrote about was business related: tracing the supply of lobster consumption in Asia. Yoyo's popular report in the China Daily News told the lobster story - from harvesting these tasty crustaceans in the North Atlantic Ocean off the Nova Scotia coast, to carefully packaging them in insulated Styrofoam containers filled with ice gel packs, to shipping the live cargo from Halifax to airports over 10,000 km away, and finally to the Chinese dining tables.....all of that being mindful of the customer's expectation that they would arrive alive.

Yoyo's new assignment also allowed him to explore the Canadian prairies and learn about the economics of the west. The reporters discovered and wrote about the "breadbasket" - Saskatchewan's innovative and high yield wheat fields. They also did reports on the massive capital investment in Northern Alberta known as the oil sands. Yoyo came to realize that he experienced parts of Canada that most Canadians never see, all in just under four years as Toronto's chief. It was quite an education. It was the essence of journalism.

Chapter 15 *A Tale of Two Marriages*

C anada, and Toronto's famously fabulous gay Village in particular, offered Yoyo many dating adventures when he was closer to his home base. The sharp contrast was not lost on him....moving from devout Tibet only a few years earlier and now living near the Village was akin to living on different planets. Yoyo felt lighter knowing that he was finally free of the emotional chains that bound him while he lived in the more conservative, image conscious China. One day after touring around the Village he confided in a friend that he felt as though he had been parachuted into the middle of his favourite disco age song: *It's Raining Men.*

Early in 2015, Yoyo was contacted by a handsome older man named Tony via one of his dating apps. Tony Pesce's profile and smiling photos caught Yoyo's attention straight away, so Yoyo agreed to meet him at Starbucks for a coffee. The fact that Yoyo detests coffee was inconsequential since he really wanted to meet this large, furry 'bear'. Tony seemed friendly and reliable....two traits that when combined are in short supply. Tony is of Italian heritage; a family oriented man, which happened to be another attribute Yoyo craves. In fact, Yo soon discovered that Tony was the only one of the three brothers who lived with his mother, keeping her company and caring for her in a North York apartment and later diligently visiting her for years in a hospital.

They talked every day, so their relationship evolved rapidly, though it never really depended on passion and sex. That was something Yoyo thought atypical but certainly not a deal breaker. Yo and Tony started to cook or dine out together once a week. Although they were both verbose they did try to adapt their communication style, working at quieting their own minds to listen to one another. They continued dating and having fun as the green shoots of spring appeared. A trip to enjoy the Montreal Pride Celebration in their first summer together brought them even closer. It seemed that Yoyo's comfort with being gay moved a more reticent Tony further along his journey of complete acceptance and, yes, pride.

For Yoyo, things seemed to be heading towards a long term commitment. Consequently, during the long ride to Montreal Pride on the transcontinental highway near Ottawa, he decided to share a big secret with his new love. Yoyo was hoping that Tony was easy-going enough to take his secret in stride, but truthfully since it was a doozy he really wasn't sure. Some might believe that telling your new Canadian boyfriend that you are going to have to leave him to spend some time in China so that you can 'marry' a lesbian girl you found on the internet is a bit off the hook. Although Tony was an experienced man in his early 40s, Yo figured his beau had probably not heard anything as odd as that plan before. He explained that he was acceding to the Chinese charade known as a Xinghun 形婚 - a staged wedding followed up with a sham marriage to appease two sets of parents. He referred to this dubious arrangement in a less disparaging term - he called it a mutual support marriage.

Since Tony had not yet seen the popular Ang Lee film *The Wedding Banquet*, Yoyo proceeded to carefully explain the Xinghun event and its incredible intricacies. If you realize this is actually trying to live two separate lives simultaneously; one with a fake partner who shows up when your family does on special occasions, and one secret life enjoying a same sex partner with whom you live with day to day, then you have arrived at the portal of figuring out this complex, yet surprisingly common, pretense.

"For some parents, it's the end of the world when their children are queer," said Fan Popo, a filmmaker, writer, and social change activist from Shandong.

In fact, one 2016 study says LGBTQ survey by the United Nations says that in China only 15% of queer people are out to family and about 5% are out at work, at their church, in other social circles. Consequently, Yoyo states that some members of China's LGBTQ community dread the Lunar New Year/holiday periods, because going home means being confronted with unwelcome questions.

Estimates are that about 16 million women in China are married to a gay man; often unbeknownst to them until the wife finds random hotel keys in the car - or gets out of bed for a late night snack and catch a glimpse of the shocking evidence from a glowing laptop in the darkness. Gay men conforming and acquiescing to social pressures to have a traditional family are nothing new, but the Xinghun sure is. The gay man seeks out and marries a lesbian woman charade is just a new cultural internet based workaround for the LGBTQ community. Since the platonic, passionless marriage seems irresponsible and actually quite cruel to the unsuspecting wife, the Xinghun idea emerged. By 2017, the largest online portal facilitating this trend claims to have "successfully matched" over 20,000 LGBTQ couples. Yoyo and his lesbian friend Ada were one of those alliances.

When the colourful leaves began their lazy descent to the ground that year, Yoyo was starting to believe that Tony could be the one - so Yo agreed to stop dating other men for a while. Tony did the same. Tony was busy managing a retail store, and Yo was still leading the Toronto news bureau. Consequently, they both worked long hours.

Therefore, they decided the only way they would see each other enough is if they could forge a plan to cohabitate. Their sexual chemistry was still evolving, but they both hoped that maybe living together would stoke the fire and lead to some passionate nights.

Around that same time, Yoyo and Tony were also busy attending to their parents' needs, in entirely different circumstances. In Toronto, Tony's mother was seriously ill, and was hospitalized in a long-term stay ward. Tony spent a lot of time after work hours with her, trying his best to work with the doctors to help her get well again. Sadly, she did not recover and passed away in December. Meanwhile, in Beijing Yoyo's parents were still healthy and serving as doting grandparents to Shen Shen, son of Meiying and the firstborn grandson of the family. Their expat son had been saving money and thinking about doing something nice for them for a long time - so Yoyo hired a realtor back in the homeland and requested that she find his parents a nice condo in the fourth or fifth ring outside the capital. He wanted their new residence to be near the subway since he wanted them to be able to get to the heart of the city as often as they desired. Within a few weeks Yoyo made a long distance condominium purchase with the intention of setting his parents up with their own place as they entered their golden years. He decided he would find a tenant to pay rent until his parents were ready to leave his sister's home.

Two months after a sublime, sun-soaked trip to Mexico together, Yoyo proposed the idea of marriage over dinner one evening during Toronto Pride 2016. Tony hesitated at first, thinking maybe his family would not accept their union. He also mulled over whether or not they had known each other long enough for that significant step. But by the end of their evening he was convinced it was the right move. They woke up the next morning and set the date: December 11th. By Canada Day they had rented out the North York Civic

Centre for the big event. Exciting things were happening. Tony and Yoyo were in love, and planning a wedding was a great antidote for the searing sadness of losing Tony's beloved mother only months earlier.

During their short engagement they took a couple of trips together, the most notable one being their hiking and sightseeing excursion to the Bruce Peninsula in central Ontario. Tony was a bit of a beach bum who loved the sun, while the slender Yoyo preferred day trips, historical landmarks and hiking. The two lovers compromised well and were able to fit both preferences into the trip itinerary. They spent time at beautiful Sauble Beach on Lake Huron. They also went cruising in the bay of Tobermory and hiked on the other side of the peninsula on the rugged Georgian Bay coastline. During that trip, Tony learned many more details of Yoyo's family dynamic, and the intense cultural pressures he was facing became crystal clear. He also learned the details of the upcoming Xinghun that Yoyo was chin deep in planning. Yoyo told Tony he would soon be away for four weeks to execute the fake marriage ruse - vowing he would be back home by mid-October. That would allow them a few more weeks to finalize the plans for the real wedding in Toronto.

On a sunny September morning, Tony drove his fiancé to the airport and wished him luck with the weird wedding. Driving home alone, Tony slipped into an unexpected sadness mixed in with a touch of anxiety. Although Tony trusted Yoyo, there were certainly moments he spent alone in his Toronto apartment when he wondered if he would ever see him again. Tony just thought that family influence might just be too much to overcome, and Yoyo would end up being forced to stay in Asia to live a life he did not want.

Meanwhile, Yo arrived in Beijing getting ready to do Xinghun with his bride Ada, a younger girl he barely knew.

The usual Xinghun routine is that the couples plan two parties, one in each of their respective hometowns. That arrangement simplifies things since the two families can be kept apart, avoiding awkward questions about the veracity of the vows. Both sets of parents seemed to believe this 'lavender' marriage was genuine and therefore were doing a lot of planning, but totally independently.

Yoyo traveled by rail to Ada's hometown for the first banquet. He was burdened with a complex mixture of emotions during his tr o....loneliness, anxiety, and shame, all mixed in with a bit of relief that very soon he would see his parents so happy at last. Even though he realized that they would not be an actual couple, or maybe because of it, Yoyo felt anxious about spending time with her family - given that he had only met Ada's parents once over dinner a few weeks earlier. Fortunately, they avoided firing any direct, unanswerable questions about the marriage in Yo's direction.

Following Chinese tradition, Yoyo was asked to show up the day before the banquet to "take" his bride, but not before playful arguments with her friends (bridesmaids in Western weddings) about what the cost of surrendering her would be. Fortunately, Yo brought along five red envelopes and filled them with 1,000 yuan each; and that seemed to suffice. They visited the banquet hall Ada's parents had rented in Fuyu county. Yoyo immediately noted that it seemed much larger than the capacity they needed from his recollection of the guest list. The room was adorned with a massive deep red area rug with traditional Chinese dragons, vines and of course phoenix. The colourful decorations were atypical of a traditional Chinese wedding, as they were mostly white and purple with charcoal gray accents. The soon to be newlywed couple smiled as the final preparations were accomplished; and dutifully played their roles better than most Hollywood actors could.

The following day it was all systems go, no surrender. The early afternoon ceremony on a breezy day turned out to be a good party, but greeting so many strangers in a six hour window certainly tested Yoyo's acting ability. Wistfully, throughout the evening he kept thinking of Tony and yearned for his life in Canada. Yo was certainly relieved when the clock struck midnight, the crowd thinned out and he could finally sneak away to send Tony a warm message. As they had hoped, Ada's mother was radiant, her father jubilant, as they finally headed home after the festivities.

A similar, but much smaller event took place the following week back in the village of Guoyuanchang where Yoyo's parents' friends gathered. At that ceremony, Yo was asked to say a few words about this bride and their goals for a life together. As he addressed the guests he made sure to assure everyone that after he completed his term in the Toronto bureau for Xinhua he would join Ada there. He made several inferences to raising children together. His parents seemed appeased, although they did not have much to say to Yoyo. After all of that, the exhausted "husband" soon bid farewell to his family and to Ada. It was October 12th, only eight weeks before his next wedding with Tony.

Indirect flights from Beijing to Toronto often last for 20-24 hours, including time spent in airports. Such a long time alone with one's thoughts is good soil for soul searching. During his trip back to Canada Yoyo had plenty of time to ponder what he had just done, and think about the lifelong commitment he was about to make with his older, same-sex partner. Although he truly believed that Tony would be a devoted husband and would make a great father, nagging concerns existed. Do I love Tony enough to commit emotionally to him for a lifetime? Will I be a good husband? How and when would I share this shocking truth with my mother and father? Will I face a temporary or permanent rift with my family? Will my needs be satisfied inside this marriage or am I likely to be unfaithful? Should I bring any or all of these concerns up to Tony prior to the wedding day? It all seemed so confusing, far more confusing than he had imagined an engagement would be.

Back in Canada, Tony greeted Yoyo at Pearson with a big hug and a stunning bouquet of roses arranged inside a Chinese bamboo plant. In the days that followed there were lots of wedding plans still to be made. Yoyo went through the motions and participated in those decisions but he still felt he needed an *ayat* - a signal; something that would speak to him from the heavens or the earth to affirm that they should actually do this deed. His sister Meiying was doing her best to counsel and support him discreetly from China, but there was just too much uncertainty rattling around in his mind. Young Yoyo decided he needed a vacation to clear his head.

Yo arrived alone in Varadero on Wednesday, the 23rd of November, 2016; which was only three short weeks prior to the next wedding. He checked into his hotel hoping to do some beach meditation, learn some communist history, take a tour of Havana, search for that elusive ayat, and make a final decision about the exchange of real vows with Tony. He decided his day trip to the iconic capital city would occur on the weekend. As he was waiting near the resort gate on Saturday morning, a doddering Havana-bound white bus approached with only a few open seats. Yoyo boarded and immediately noted the somber mood amongst many of the locals, the Latino passengers. Many were sobbing, a few uncontrollably. The seat he took was across the aisle from a Caucasian couple who seemed more serene. That afforded him the opportunity to speak in English to try to find out what all the sadness was about. In a hushed voice, the woman told Yoyo why most of Cuba was plunged into mourning.

His mind was racing.....*Two days after arriving for his only visit to Cuba, is the death of an iconic, revered and simultaneously despised leader like Fidel Castro classified as an ayat?*

On his bus trip through the mostly barren countryside, Yoyo had very spotty phone signals. However, he was able to discern that former President Castro passed away just before midnight; and he began to realize just how historic this event was for Cuban residents and the 1.5 million strong who had fled their homeland. Suddenly, his trip to Havana seemed a great deal spicier. While most of the other passengers looked at this event through the lens of how this would shape their future as residents of one of the last communist countries, Yoyo was mulling over whether or not Castro's passing was a marriage message from the heavens. And if it was, what exactly was that message?

Old Havana has stunning old architecture, and is the part of the city that looks as though it was frozen in 1970. Vedado, in contrast, is the much more commercialized section of the capital, although it would never be confused with Manhattan or Toronto. Yoyo spent most of his time taking pictures in Revolution Square where tens of thousands of Cubans gathered to mourn Castro, before he rushed to Old Havana, taking more photos and walking as briskly as he could to maximize his time there. He walked over 10km that day, and treated himself to a nice restaurant meal on a patio as the sun set. Yoyo finished his rosé and realized he had to figure out where and when to find the last bus. Since he initially thought that la salida *(departure)* referred to local cuisine, he almost missed it. Eventually he climbed aboard the bus and found a window seat well after darkness had fallen and stars had risen. The weary traveler finally had some quiet time to reflect on his very eventful day. Just before the bus crept up to the hotel entrance, Yoyo decided he would indeed marry Tony as planned - with the added bonus of embarking on another, much longer journey. He would tell h s new husband that he really wanted to try to raise a family together.

Yoyo arrived home from Cuba a mere 12 days before their wedding day. Fortunately, not much more planning needed to be completed, since this would be a small affair and only Tony's family and a few friends would attend. The guest list totaled 39 people. In the days prior to that wedding Yoyo was able to keep his emotions under control, and dutifully tried to keep his man calm, but to no avail. Tony was certainly excited about finally finding his life partner, but he was also dealing with some internal angst about the varying levels of tolerance, acceptance, and genuine happiness he was faced with from his Italian family members. To complicate matters, he was still lamenting the loss of his mother, and of course his mind drifted there, wishing she could be his rock prior to the wedding. Tears flowed and abundant hearty hugs soothed his pain.

A smattering of lily white oversized snowflakes danced towards the ground early on the morning of December 11th as Tony enjoyed his expresso. As the clock approached 8 he waited patiently in the living area for his sleeping beauty, alone with his thoughts of the big day ahead. Tony thought about how much more comfortable he now was as a gay man, how authentic his life had become since falling in love with Yoyo. He enjoyed the scent of his coffee as he hummed along as Boyzone's lovely lyric played softly on the speaker beside him…

'I can't deny what I believe, I can't be what I'm not.'

He felt a sense of calm as he anticipated their first dance together as the band played on….

'I know this love's forever, that's all that matters now no matter what.'

His eyes were still moist when Yoyo suddenly approached, looked into his big hazel eyes, and gave him a very warm embrace.

Chapter 16 *Benevolence Betrayed*

P rior to getting hitched Yoyo met some gay men in the Village and via matchmaking sites like Grindr & Growlr. Some of those people were genuine and eminently datable, but several others clearly were not and were quickly cast aside - though it would be more accurate to say that all but one of them were quickly dismissed. Carlos Santos, a 49 year old vagabond and unsuccessful artist entered Yoyo's life and turned it upside down shortly thereafter. After having a brief conversation and impulsive exchange of digits with Santos at a bar on Church Street one night, Yoyo went home alone as usual. Nonetheless, he was so bored the following day so he decided to reply to Santos' uninspired "What up man?" text message. After some shallow, flirtatious banter, he agreed to a first date with Carlos later that week. Both decisions were destined to linger on Yoyo like skunk spray.

After several weeks of lackluster conversations and a few uneventful restaurant dates where Carlos was always in the washroom when the bill arrived, Yoyo soon realized that Carlos was not nteresting enough, not successful enough, and appeared to be too neurotic to be in any sort of relationship with. He wanted to keep searching. However, for reasons that became inexplicable later, Yoyo felt some unexpected sympathy for Carlos. Shortly before what was expected to be a farewell conversation, a benevolent thought occurred to Yo....maybe I should offer Carlos the guest room as a tenant and roommate for a few months until he gets his career back on track. Carlos seemed grateful and quickly accepted the offer: which was a month to month rental agreement at only $300 per month rent plus buy his own food. The skunk was getting closer.

As Halloween approached that year, Carlos had been in the guest room for almost a year, making all his rent payments despite his lack of employment. For a few months Yoyo had even "hired" Carlos to help him with providing ideas and research for some of his news reports. However, his tenant had started to frustrate Yoyo in various ways, with his late night habits, and due to the unwelcome friends staying who kept staying overnight on the couch. One fateful day Yoyo was cleaning and found the old work laptop he had gifted to Carlos powered on with the desktop in view. He noted that one of the folders was titled with the name Yan, so his curiosity led him to check out what exactly Carlos was collecting. As he began opening files Yoyo's heart started to race and his mind became cluttered with a mix of rage and confusion.....he discovered a mosaic of photo images of Yo's credit cards, driver's license, passport and several other work related documents. What is this all about? Is Carlos a thief? Taking advantage of my kindness? What should I do?

That evening Yo confronted his traitorous tenant and told him that he had confiscated the loaned laptop. He was furious. He kicked him out on the spot; but not before telling him that he would be monitoring his credit cards and watching for anything that looked fraudulent. Yoyo felt so much anger and disbelief since he had been so kind to his unemployed "friend". A distressing betrayal is often a painful lesson. Nonetheless, after a few weeks passed with no indications of credit card fraud or other identity theft, Yoyo, who was by then living alone, was able to refocus on his affairs and be productive again. Although he was shaken by what had occurred, he truly believed that the sickening skunk was out of his life forever.

Hold on Tight

Unfortunately, he would soon learn otherwise.

Chapter 17 *Holding on Tight*

I mmediately after Yoyo and Tony exchanged their vows they began their new lives together in a cozy apartment in north Toronto's Tobermory Drive, a few steps away from Finch Avenue. Tony continued to work in the grocery business for an Italian retailer in Vaughan, and the plan for Yoyo was that he would play the role of home organizer while he worked on finding a new job. He had left the Chinese news agency job prior to his trip to China to lavender wed Ada. However, as famous boxer Mike Tyson once stated at a press conference....

"You know everyone has a plan, until life punches you in the face."

So as the ink was still drying on their marriage certificate, nine days before Christmas Yoyo took a call from Beijing with a demand that felt like a punch to the face. An executive from Human Resources called Yoyo to tell him that his time as their Toronto Bureau Chief was now under investigation. He was told that the Toronto office had received a letter from an unnamed source with an accusation of embezzlement - a term which Yoyo did not immediately recognize as meaning internal financial crimes. The HR representative did not share many specifics on the call, but instead declared that he would follow up with a more formal request by email the next day. Yoyo was perplexed and despondent that only three months after returning to Canada and six short days into his marriage, he would have to return to China for an unknown duration. When he asked the Xinhua caller how long he would need to be in China, the reply was not comforting. He was told it would be at least one month, and likely longer.

When the email arrived the following morning, Yoyo was anxious to read the details before breaking his bad news to Tony. Some additional facts about the investigation were listed as follows:

- In October a letter from someone named "Carl" had been sent to Xinhua HQ
- The letter stated that Carl's former roommate, a man named Yan, had boasted about misdirecting thousands of dollars from his employer
- The letter stated that more details of this alleged embezzling could be found on Facebook
- The investigation was now 45 days old, and it was necessary for Yoyo to face in person interrogations, providing answers to questions posed by Xinhua's legal department in Beijing.

Yoyo was in shock as he tried to process all of this new information. He replied that he had nothing to hide but needed some time to consider his options. He promised that he would follow up and confirm his level of participation in the inquiry within two days. He managed to gather himself enough to prepare dinner for Tony, crack open a bottle of red, and await his husband's arrival home so they could respond and plan a pathway forward. The plan was that Yoyo would make arrangements to leave Toronto in early January and return by Valentine's Day.

When Yoyo reported back to Xinhua offices he was summoned into a room where three different representatives from different departments laid out the details of the embezzlement accusations. None of them were accurate, and Yo offered his full cooperation.

He was so certain of his innocence that he pledged a 100,000 yuan bond that would be available for any financial reimbursement that his bosses felt necessary. Fortunately, by the end of April, the investigation was shuttered and their ruling was that no discernible money was missing or misspent. Yoyo received his 100k back and was told his employment was terminated. Getting "fired" seemed odd to Yo considering he had submitted his resignation to those same people before the wedding season began four months earlier; combined with the fact that the Toronto news bureau had actually closed on January 1st. The termination letter from Xinhua's HR department was clearly a power play, a bit of Chinese gamesmanship intended to save face and possibly even to harm his future employability. While shaken by his former employer's mistrust, Yoyo was just happy to be free to leave China and begin a new chapter of his life with his husband; having survived the sabotage attempt.

Meanwhile in Toronto, Tony tried to ignore a friend and some close family members who were dubious of the whole situation, and mentioned that they felt Tony should move on. They planted seeds of doubt about Yoyo's planned return to Canada and his true intentions. Tony continued to have faith in his husband in absentia, despite the naysayers. He too was **holding on tight.**

Chapter **18**   *The Baby Project*

Y oyo was finally able to catch a flight back to Canada on the last day of April 2017, almost four months after leaving Toronto to deal with the investigation. Finally, married life could begin.

Upon their reunion, Tony had the lasagna and red wine ready to go as he welcomed his husband home with much relief and raw emotion. For the first few months the new couple were quite harmonious. Yoyo was unemployed as he had no work status in Canada; but he found ways to keep busy through their first summer and autumn together. Their matrimonial condominium was previously owned by Tony's mom and consequently her collection of mementos were scattered about, so Yo spent his time culling old trinkets and reorganizing their living space. Tony continued to work long hours at the store. After a few months at home alone for 10-12 hours a day, boredom was the inevitable outcome for someone like Yoyo. Spending money like a sailor in port became his focus; but the attempt at retail therapy updating Tony's wardrobe was only a temporary tonic for that boredom.

Yoyo had two prior ties as that summer slowly faded into a colourful autumn in north Toronto. His main focus was seeking legal status, known as permanent residency (PR) in Canada. Although many immigrants who marry Canadians would pursue the spousal sponsorship, Yoyo chose a different path, leveraging his Canadian work experience. As is customary, his PR application mandated a Canadian Security Intelligence Service (CSIS)* clearance.

Kevin McCaffrey

CSIS is Canada's Intelligence agency on matters relating to national security - meaning it conducts national security investigations and many forms of intelligence collection. CSIS collects and analyzes intelligence, and reports to the Government of Canada on any and all activities that may threaten Canada and its citizens.

CSIS requested Yoyo attend two separate interviews to learn more about his time in Canada working with Xinhua - the biggest news agency/arm of the Chinese Communist Party. They interrogated Yoyo on the veracity of his activities in Islamabad and in Kabul, seemingly to ensure he was only there as a legitimate journalist. A comprehensive investigation of the Yan file lasted for over 24 months - during which time Yoyo had to wait patiently without employment. Eventually the Canadian authorities determined that there was nothing suspicious about his past, and he attained full PR status and would be able to resume his career.

That time without any legal status gave Yo plenty of time to work on his second priority, having a family. The newlyweds decided that their first foray into the world of surrogacy would be by trying the traditional approach. They were seeking a woman who would agree to be inseminated with either husband's seed to fertilize her egg during ovulation, carry the baby to term, and ultimately be comfortable enough to relinquish that baby to the intended parents without regret. Quite clearly the biggest question was: who could they trust with such an important mission? They quickly answered that query with a second, rhetorical question: If she were willing and able, who could possibly be a better choice for this magnanimous act than one's pretend wife?

After a few months of dialogue back and forth across the Pacific, Ada and her lesbian partner Zoe agreed to join Yoyo and Tony in Canada as surrogate mothers. The agreement was kept top secret in their respective families to avoid the wrath of shocked parents. It was a verbal deal that included free room and board for the birth mothers and $50,000CAD each as compensation for their time and efforts - since the girls would try to deliver not one but **two** babies at North York General.

Ada and Zoe arrived in Canada on tourist visas in March of 2018. They settled into the guest room in the cozy apartment. Yoyo kept them busy during the day and then cooked some delicious Chinese dishes to make them feel closer to home. Since there are only three fertile days each month to transform a precious egg into a zygote, that provided the Chinese visitors with loads of time to travel around Ontario and beyond, with Yoyo usually serving as their tour guide. The girls were treated to several nice road trips, including a visit to Niagara Falls, taking a tour of the Thousand Islands area - and the two couples even spent a week in balmy Miami, FL.

IVF Canada had to give them medical clearance as healthy women who could bear children. After 45 days that goal was achieved, and the fearless foursome fired off several attempts at sexless insemination. Sadly, before a pregnancy came to be, an unexpected misalignment of mutual expectations occurred. Surrogacy is a complex process so it can be rife with emotional sensitivity, for obvious reasons. In this case Ada and Zoe felt that they were not being treated as real family; rather they became dismayed about the transactional nature of their visit. For a few days they kept quiet about their feelings, but one night between the stir fry and the espresso Ada boldly aired her grievance at the dinner table. Additionally, several disagreements and insidious accusations of the host couple's tight-fistedness started to surface. The girls were frustrated and stated their dissatisfaction with various things that Tony and Yoyo decided not to purchase, and some disdain for some things they did purchase that were deemed to be too cheap. Although they were slow to allow themselves to admit and discuss this issue, eventually it became apparent to Yoyo and Tony that their baby agreement was starting to come apart at the seams.

One day in July Tony found Yoyo in tears when he arrived home. Their guests had finally pushed Yoyo too far, and Tony stepped in to intervene. The hosts were angry and decided that Ada and Zoe should spend a week in a hotel alone, to truly consider their commitment to the entire project. Seven days later, they still couldn't see eye to eye. Therefore, the four of them decided to withdraw from the agreement and move on. Ada, the lavender bride, ended all communication with Yoyo.

Chapter 19 *Life with Tony & Mac*

Y oyo and Tony were both upset about that turn of events, but in actuality Yo was far beyond upset - he was devastated. Those next few weeks felt to Yoyo as if he was falling into the depths of the valley of doom. Tony provided tremendous support when he wasn't working, but as much as he tried he could not ease his partner's pain alone. Fortunately, Yo was becoming more adept at social networking. Consequently, only three months after the girls bailed out, he connected with a gay Facebook group that gave him new hope. Some of his new online acquaintances showed off their family photos and told compelling stories about their successful surrogacy journeys. One couple in particular chatted with Yoyo frequently and became de facto mentors for the hopeful parents as they considered next steps. That couple recommended that Yo and Tony meet with a fertility clinic and explore the process of being "matched" with a motivated gestational carrier (woman). A few weeks later, late in 2018, the two husbands signed a contract with the Friendly Fertility Clinic (FFC), and learned about the requirements, the process, and the probability of outcomes.

One of the first steps to FFC's process was finding an egg "donor". Once that mission was accomplished the hopeful parents would be asked to come to the renowned CReATe fertility clinic in Toronto and release their "soldiers" for immediate deep freeze storage. A sister company to the FFC was willing to assist and ultimately helped Yoyo find an anonymous 25 year old healthy woman from the Cambridge area who agreed to offer her help. She was summoned to the clinic to harvest her eggs in one cycle, which would in turn be used to create several PGS-tested embryos for Tony and Yoyo as the couple shared the fertilization process. In the end, the three "healthiest" zygotes were kept and carefully frozen at the clinic. All that was needed next was a suitable surrogate birth mother - and lots of luck.

Meanwhile, 3,800 km away, an energetic puppy entered the world in a litter of 10 near San Miguel de Allende, Mexico. Thanks to dog rescue organizations in both Mexico and Canada and the tireless efforts of good people such as Canadian snowbirds Barbara and Bill Estabrooks, abandoned dogs can get a second chance at a good life. In Mac's case, he was found and rescued from the street alone and frightened – so Mac ended up on the San Miguel dog shelter website. Barbara was nearing the end of her annual winter pilgrimage to San Miguel and came across his photo and went to the shelter to meet him. Within days she arranged to adopt Mac, and took him to a local vet who provided the necessary paperwork. Barbara brought Mac to Canada at the end of March as a five month old rambunctious puppy. That was the third year Barbara had brought a dog home with her, and the second time she did so with the intention of fostering him while searching for a permanent home.

Yoyo and Tony were still eager to have a family, and as fortune would have it they heard about Barbara & Mac's return to Canada through a friend. When they saw Mac on their first FaceTime call it was love at first sight. After some and assurances to Barbara that they would take great care of him, Yoyo and Tony officially became Mac's owners on May 10th, 2019. While both husbands enjoyed the addition to their family, Yoyo was especially grateful to have a canine companion given all the time he spent alone in the apartment. The next few months were an adventure to be sure. Acclimating Mac to their home was not easy, but the couple showered Mac with affection, even as his sharp little teeth nibbled on every finger and toe within reach. Their heartwarming puppy parenting experience firmly validated their yearning to become parents.

The Friendly Fertility Clinic contract stipulated that a suitable surrogate woman from their database would be introduced to clients within 12 months. By the end of October 2019, that promise was unfulfilled - and Yoyo was getting extremely frustrated by the delay. The $15,000 initial payment to get the ball rolling had produced virtually nothing. Some of the frustration also arose from the palpable pressure from Yoyo's traditionalist parents, who still whole-heartedly believed he had married a woman and was fully capable of making them proud grandparents.

Traditional Confucian beliefs and embedded filial piety allows for, and in some subcultures even mandates, parents to have great influence in their adult children's lives. In its healthiest form, filial piety will honour and thank parents for the sacrifices they have made to provide for one's needs. It is a value passed from generation to generation, to respect those that came before. Respecting and loving one's parents is certainly a mainstream global expectation; and reciprocal types of this sort of piety can indeed be healthy - **if** the parents can accept and even nurture the individuality of a child. Sadly, in Asia, coercing and shaming children to do things for blind loyalty too often creeps into families; which can lead to conflicts. The effect on the child can certainly vary, but this coercion almost always comes with the expectation of conformity, without any thought or regard for a son or daughter's sexuality. Even choosing to move to another continent was only a temporary respite for the angst of the Yan's only son.

As he approached his 38th birthday Yoyo still struggled with the decision about disclosing his sexuality to his parents. He spent countless hours thinking about some version of this vexing question: *is this the right time to come out of the closet and unmask myself?* It didn't help that Tony was equally nervous about the impact of that disclosure. Mostly in jest, Tony occasionally spoke about his concern that his new mother-in-law might be hostile enough to chop him up and make him into a Chinese dumpling when she discovered their marriage. Yoyo sought to be reassuring through this period, telling Tony that his mother would not even perceive their marriage to be real. In fact, Yoyo told him that his mother did not personally know of any same sex marriages; and the whole concept was just beyond her comprehension. Consequently, Yoyo and Tony made a plan. They would live together but Tony would never be mentioned or seen in the background during any of Yoyo's video calls with his family. As soon as their first pregnancy was successful, Yo would immediately follow that joyous news by revealing the truth about his sexuality and marriage. He would finally stop kicking that can down the road. He would try to cushion the 'bad' news with some wonderful news.

Being matched up with and fertilizing a surrogate woman proved to be far more challenging than the hopeful parents could have imagined. It became apparent that some candidates had registered with the agency without a true commitment to following through. Their commendable sense of altruism is too often derailed for one reason or another; including inadequate husband support, the many medical and clinical appointments required, or conflicts that arise with the intended parents. As it turned out, the two women that they were introduced to over that 12 month period were not very motivated, and the clock was ticking.

In hindsight, the numerous baby project setbacks created irritability, some tension and emotional distance within the marriage. Not that it was either partner's fault, but

FFC's inability to come through for them started to really affect Yoyo's moods, and romance became more infrequent. Laughter, a surefire prescription for what ails a marriage, was absent for most of 2019.

Since becoming a couple they had enjoyed many nights roaming around the V lage, people watching and hanging out at Woody's for the drag shows and best bum contests. It was one of their favourite forms of socialization. As they made their journey downtown one Saturday evening when Yoyo was at a low poirt, he and Tony made an agreement as they talked about their dwindling passion. They both agreed that they wanted to inject a spark into their sex lives, by occasionally looking for hot new friends in the Gay Village and online. They both updated their profiles on the gay dating sites from status "married" to "married seeking more".

On one late summer night downtown in their favourite bar, Yoyo and Tony started chatting up an off duty police officer named Matt, who briefly excused himself to go and find his partner Steven so they could all get to know one another. Matt was slightly taller than Yoyo, and Yo immediately noted his broad shoulders and muscular, hard body. After he found out about Yoyo's lifelong attraction to men in uniform, Matt teased him by showing a couple of photos while on duty in his full cop kit. Yoyo was trying to hide his attraction to Matt, but not very successfully. Tony, a great guy and not one for conflict, found Yoyo's yearning more amusing than annoying. Besides, his attention was diverted to the younger man on *his* radar. Steven, age 25 with a more slender build, smooth skin, and an impressive shock of saw-tooth spiked black hair, was much quieter than his outgoing partner. He flashed a cute half smile that he seemed to be trying to suppress, but it revealed itself a few times as they all chatted. Tony quickly became smitten. After the conversation and fun ended at Woody's the flirtatious foursome headed down the street to their favourite coffee shop for more banter and policing stories. Although no partner swapping occurred that night and the couples went their separate ways well after 2:00 a.m., the vodka and a foundation for future fun had both been poured.

Yoyo found himself thinking about Matt & Steven often during his daily dog walks. He and Tony had not really talked much about the details of their "seeking more" agreement so Yo perceived this particular opportunity as a blank canvas.

Questions needed to be answered......

Where should we do this?

Should we suggest a foursome or is it better to pair up with separate rooms?

What should be permitted and what sex acts would cross the line?

Yoyo and Matt used WhatsApp to discuss a plan, and Yo relayed the information to Tony. Yoyo and his Italian stallion were equally stoked about their first foray outside their marriage. During discussions Matt disclosed that he and Steven were seasoned veterans in this milieu, having enjoyed several fun sessions over the preceding years. As a member of the Toronto Police Service for over 20 years Matt was entitled to ample time off work, and he told Yoyo that he sometimes used his vacations to adventure travel to countries in Asia. Yoyo was impressed.

The double date was confirmed. Two weeks later the four of them met for drinks at a cozy bar near Matt & Steven's place and then went on to their house for the much awaited mayhem. Matt and Steven enjoyed their spirits and preferred intimacy with a good buzz while their guests had a preference for sobriety. After their hosts put back several vodka and tonics, the couples split up for the drive to Matt's place - Tony drove Steven and Yoyo drove Matt *a la casa.*

The host's three bedroom, modest home was beautifully decorated, mostly in Asian themes. Steven, who grew up in Hong Kong and immigrated to Canada for his post-secondary studies, showed them around and clearly had a flair for interior design. He found work in Canada after graduation and met/fell in love with the much older Matt in the summer of 2016 - they had been together for three years. Although Matt did most of the talking, the hosts seemed quite at ease with one another, giving off a comforting aura of *simpatico.* After the brief house tour concluded, Matt emerged from the master bedroom and joined the other three in the living room. Yoyo looked up and his eyes widened immediately. Matt was shirtless and wearing only his white jockstrap.

"I changed into something a bit more comfortable," Matt said playfully.

A brief silence was followed by Steven's giggles before Tony mustered the courage to say:

"Nice outfit. Did you find that in the Village?"

As Matt nodded and gave a one word affirmation, he took a seat in his oversized recliner.

"Care to join me?" he asked as he locked eyes with Yoyo.

A few hours later on the drive home Yoyo and Tony chatted about what had transpired. Reticent to disclose too many details initially, they began discussing the new dynamic in their sex lives. Yoyo confessed that he had just satisfied a lifelong yearning to be intimate with a burly police officer. He told Tony not to worry; Matt was not emotionally invested and most likely not into anything more than a one-time hook up - at least that was the vibe he received once their steamy session ended. Tony, for his part, was unfazed since he was still basking in the afterglow of his time spent with Steven. He told Yoyo that he and Steven were uncomfortable with how to get their little tryst started, but eventually they did have some fun. He mentioned that Steven was very tactile and also a talented kisser. Tony stated that he thought Yoyo was misreading the situation with Matt, and he remained optimistic there would be more naughty nights with their new friends. What they did not discuss that night were any specific sex acts and acceptable boundaries.

Chapter 20 *A Fork in the Road*

O ver the next few weeks Yoyo was still unable to work, so he ramped up his activity on his two favourite gay dating sites. He changed the relationship status field from married to *open*. One day nearing the end of September, Yo received a brief message from a guy whose profile was titled DaBulldog. The message DaBulldog sent was a compliment about Yo's profile picture, where he was sitting on a lovely Caribbean beach drinking from a coconut shell. Yoyo replied and within a few days he and Kirk (DaBulldog) had set up a first meeting for a game of tennis followed by a drink in Kirk's backyard.

Unbeknownst to his potential suitor, Yoyo was undergoing a low point in his life and was looking for a friend as much as a lover. He arrived at Kirk's home with a lot on his mind - eager to talk to someone in an attempt to unburden himself. Kirk poured his guest a glass of wine and invited Yoyo to join him on the deck. About an hour later, Yoyo finished talking about his frustrations with the delay in getting status in Canada, the unsuccessful baby project, spending so much time alone due to Tony's job, and a few other less significant concerns. Kirk listened, listened some more, and tried to offer some perfunctory support for his visitor. During a bathroom break Kirk disappeared into the house, spending a few extra minutes trying to decide if he was interested in pursuing this friendship or not. He decided to return to the table, but since the discussion had been so focused on Yoyo and his problems, Kirk redirected the conversation so that he could tell Yoyo a bit about his life.

Eventually, a decision had to be made about tennis before any more wine was consumed, so Kirk mentioned that he had two racquets and some new balls if Yoyo still wanted to play. Cheekily, Yoyo smiled and dropped a strong hint that he was in the mood to play, but tennis could wait.

Before moving inside Yoyo told Kirk that he and his partner had an ongoing agreement to have casual fun dates outside their marriage. He mentioned that he had informed Tony that morning that he would be heading out for an afternoon delight. So, a few minutes later, Yoyo and Kirk found themselves in a warm embrace. They undressed one another and spent a while between some satin sheets. After their pleasure session ended Yoyo had a quick shower and then thanked Kirk for his hospitality. He excused himself with the explanation that he had promised to prepare a nice dinner for Tony. The new friends agreed that they could try to find time to play tennis the following weekend.

When Yoyo returned home late that afternoon Tony was busy watching his beloved football team, the Buffalo Bills. Yoyo prepared a chicken and sticky rice dish – and after the game they dined together. Observing that his husband was happier than in previous days, Tony asked him about the afternoon date and who he was with. Yoyo stated that he had met someone older that he found attractive, and that they had made tentative plans to get together the following weekend to play tennis. When Tony asked if Yoyo had fun, Yoyo knew exactly what he meant and answered in the affirmative, but that line of inquiry ended abruptly.

Less than a week later, after 28 months of waiting for the government bureaucracy to do their thing, Yoyo's coveted permanent residency notification finally arrived. Yet another milestone for Yoyo Yan, the "PR" would allow him to have full legal status to work for in Canada. All of the uncertainty of the government's looming decision was replaced with relief that Canada accepted him. An enormous emotional burden had been lifted from his shoulders at last. Optimism and joy had returned to Yoyo's life.

Yoyo and Kirk did not see each other as planned the following weekend. Their next meeting occurred on a chilly Monday in January after Kirk had returned from a vacation. Yoyo suggested that they use two of his soon expiring admission tickets to visit the Royal Ontario Museum (ROM) together. When they arrived to find the ROM closed, they changed course and ate lunch at Asian Legend in Chinatown. During their long walkabout in the city, Yoyo talked about his family, his formative years studying English at Chengdu, his time in Tibet, and his international journalism experiences. Kirk noted that Yoyo's life to date was unique and full of twists and turns. He became quite intrigued. Yoyo seemed flattered by the attention. They concluded their date thinking that they would continue to see one another occasionally.

Kirk and Yoyo were both considering new car purchases in the coming year, so in early February Yoyo made arrangements for some media passes and the new friends headed downtown to check out the auto show. It was after that event, while having drinks at Jack Astor's bar, when Yoyo realized that he may have an unexpected dilemma to deal with…..he was falling in love with Kirk. Yoyo did not sleep well that night. He was only sure of one thing as he wrestled with his confusing and conflicted thoughts - *he knew that he did not want to hurt Tony but he also did not want to stop seeing Kirk.* How to accomplish those two perilous objectives kept Yoyo awake until the first rays of sunlight peeked through the blinds.

Meanwhile, as March approached and an invisible enemy known as Covid 19 virus began its wicked impact on

Canadian life, it became a lonely time for people who were single, as the scary virus pumped the brakes on dating new people. Due to the fact that Yoyo was married and had his plans to start a family with Tony, Kirk told Yoyo he viewed the arrangement as 'friends with benefits'. Kirk continued to date a nubile nurse during the early months of 2020, but he always made time for Yoyo.

Back in North York, Yoyo and Tony continued to message and respond to a bevy of profiles of attractive guys they found on their dating sites. When it became apparent to Tony that his partner had less and less interest in chatting and arranging dates with new men, he deduced that it was because of Yoyo's interest in Kirk. Consequently, Tony and Yoyo had their first dispute when Tony made reference to the evolving situation. Their argument was brief but Tony clearly said that his preference would be that any future fun the two of them would have outside the marriage should be together, and he wasn't happy with all the Kirk talk occurring in their home. Yoyo suggested that if it would make Tony feel better, and in an ongoing attempt to be honest and transparent about the nature of their friendship, they could invite his new friend to their home for dinner. Tony agreed, and started to think about what he wanted to say (and not say) to Kirk and Yoyo when the opportunity arose.

By the time February came to a close, Yoyo was seeing Kirk about once a week and Tony was spending most of his time working and browsing through dating sites. Yoyo approached the subject carefully but eventually extended the dinner invitation to Kirk - with the pitch that Tony was a terrific cook and would prepare a special Italian dish for them. Kirk told Yoyo he wasn't sure it was a great idea, but after thinking it over they agreed that it would be best for everyone to meet and figure out the best way forward. Much to Tony's relief Kirk was very clear that he had no motivation to marry, that he was happy living alone, and admitted that he may have misunderstood their play with others arrangement. For his part, Tony wanted to meet Kirk so that he could clarify the terms of their agreement face to face and with all present. Yoyo brokered the "deal" and a potentially turbulent dinner date was planned for the following Saturday.

Kirk showed up as planned. After their very cordial dinner ended, the three men settled into the living area with some Baileys on ice. Things got awkward fast. Tony took a deep breath and broke the silence as Yoyo sat on the arm of his chair and gently stroked his arm. Tony wanted to tell their guest that regardless of anything Yoyo may have said or inferred, their marriage was not an "open" relationship - rather it was a deal where the partners could have occasional hook-ups or preferably play together in threesomes. As time passed, Tony began to speak very emotionally and with increased volume. Yoyo continued to try to comfort and support his husband with touches and reassuring words as Tony continued. To Yoyo's relief, Kirk was mostly silent except for some verbal affirmations of understanding. Finally, Tony stated firmly that the main reason he was willing to meet his husband's new lover was to establish clear rules and boundaries going forward. When Tony paused and appeared to have said all he had to say, Yoyo spoke briefly but Tony seemed to dismiss his pleas. Eventually, Kirk found an opening to speak. He tried to empathize and apologize for the misunderstanding. He told Tony that he understood his angst. He took a deep breath, looked at Yoyo first and then into Tony's dilated eyes and said that it was likely best that he and Yoyo not see each other in person to avoid the risk of more misunderstandings. Yoyo was not happy with that comment, but remained silent.

Their visitor seemed to sense that the couple needed their space and decided to head home. Yoyo and Tony continued their discussion after their guest departed. Ten minutes later Yoyo and Tony called Kirk, who picked up the unexpected call in the car before he even arrived home. Apparently, the partners had reached a compromise and Yoyo explained that Tony had decided that some tennis games, nights out together and even occasional fun would be acceptable. As Tony explained his evolving thoughts a bit more using speakerphone, Kirk listened intently as he tried to ponder the whole situation. He said that he was surprised and was in no hurry to see either of them again.

As it turned out, Yoyo and Kirk saw one another once every couple of weeks in March and April, often hiking together with Mac and playing sports together. Yoyo wanted to learn how to play hockey, and Kirk was happy to find him some skates and put him on the ice. They became quite close during that time, but Yoyo was still committed to having his marriage and starting a family with Tony. He kept reminding himself, and Kirk of his improbable mantra..... *I don't want to hurt Tony but I don't want to lose you either.* The winds of change were starting to blow, but the storm was still some distance away.

By late April, Tony was becoming less and less enthusiastic about their *"seeking more"* agreement. After a couple of weeks of tension and some arguments about how and when they should be allowed to spend time with other men, Yoyo decided he needed a break.....they called it a trial separation. Yoyo left his home, not knowing how he would feel without Tony by his side. Yoyo was still working at Freemont and having trouble focusing on his news reports; while back in north Toronto Tony was not sleeping well and sought some advice from his brothers. Tony and Yoyo continued to message each other and spoke on the phone to try to find common ground to go forward in peace. Tears and wine both flowed when they reconnected the following weekend after their hiatus. It was evident to both of them that they loved each other deeply, but Yoyo came to the conclusion that his love had evolved.

The month of May was less tumultuous and more exciting, because with Tony's assistance Yoyo was shopping for his first new vehicle, and by mid-month he was driving a fully loaded, metallic blue Jeep. The joy of buying and driving Yoyo's dream car helped soothe some of the pain caused by their marital strife. Tony and Yoyo continued to talk daily, trying to put things back together. Yoyo was asking for a true open relationship going forward, and negotiations on that front continued for a few weeks before falling apart. No agreement was reached, and the situation became bleak.

By June of 2020, the global Covid 19 pandemic hit Canada hard and everyone was on edge, watching the horrible impact on senior citizens, nursing homes and immunocompromised individuals. The tension of those times may have played a role in the husband's decision to separate. Yoyo and Mac left their home in Toronto one Sunday afternoon. Yoyo drove north, and was greeted with a hug as he asked if he could move some of his things into Kirk's small home.

Chapter 21 *The Honey Badger*

A few months earlier, on an otherwise dreary winter day in the last week of 2019, Freemont Media had contacted Yoyo with a response to a job interview he had done five weeks earlier. It was a vacancy that he had assumed had already been filled, so he was pleasantly surprised to find the belated offer in his inbox.

"We are pleased to be able to inform you that you are the successful candidate for the Senior News Reporter position at Freemont Media. As discussed previously, this is a full time contract position. If you choose to accept our offer you will be compensated at a rate of $3,000 monthly, and will be paid bi-weekly on Fridays. Benefits would commence after a 3 month probationary period ends. We need you to begin work in our Markham bureau on or before January 13, 2020. Please contact Doris Au-Yeung in our HR department for more details. She can be reached at dorisay@freemontmedia.ca"

After an evening of contemplation and a quick discussion with Tony, Yoyo contacted the HR rep and accepted the job. Although the salary level was only about half of what he believed he was worth, Yoyo realized that he just needed a ticket into the dance, and after being admitted in he could likely find a more attractive dance partner. After years of waiting and various immigration related and job search disappointments, the honey badger had his first job working for a Canadian employer!

Yoyo ended his hiatus from journalism and began working again. His first two weeks were uneventful, but he found the workload stressful since his boss, Anderson, was proving to be an annoying micromanager. At Freemont,

Yoyo was creating news reports for a Mandarin channel - doing video montages with voiceovers - then submitting his work daily at 4:00 p.m. for review. Virtually every day, Anderson would find an inconsequential "flaw" with the work of his nine reporters. Although the workday was supposed to end by 5:30, Anderson's staff often stayed up to 90 minutes late, painstakingly editing to please him. Yoyo noticed that none of the reporters, most of whom were young and lacking experience elsewhere, voiced any displeasure about this often unnecessary, inefficient day-to-day routine. Yo decided that he would just try to adjust his daily expectations, stay silent, and never make any firm dinner plans.

Months passed and Yoyo was doing his best to write stories for the nightly news broadcast. Unfortunately, those first few months at Freemont coincided with the most challenging time of his marriage. The combined stressors of juggling his demanding boss, an increasingly distant marriage, the ongoing parental pressures, and occasional flare-ups with Tony were weighing on Yoyo - especially in sharp contrast with all of the free time he enjoyed during most of his brief marriage. In addition, finding time to chat with and see Kirk was also really becoming important to him in the early months of 2020. Even badgers need to rest sometimes.

Consequently, after only four months working at Freemont, Yoyo was getting increasingly dissatisfied with the rigid culture, and more specifically the tense environment Tuesdays through Saturdays when Anderson was Newsroom Manager. The other two days were more pleasurable, when a more easy-going boss was steering the ship. After being subjected to two public, dubious criticisms of his work habits and the quality of his voice, it became clear to Yoyo that this untenable situation must simply become a stepping stone to his next job. Then, on an otherwise uneventful Friday in June, the fur *really* started to fly.

Manager Anderson was doing his rounds, which too often involved interrupting the workflow and asking about the journalist's progress on their stories. On this particular day, as he hovered between three reporters desks he made a derogatory comment about Chinese accents. It was an ill-advised but brief comment, one which normally would have been ignored if not for it offending a nearby reporter who was born in that region of China, and who was known to pronounce certain words differently than most of his colleagues. Yoyo made the mistake of validating his bosses' comment and added his own thoughts while they had a quick laugh about the difference in dialects. Apparently the colleague who spoke that way had heard enough. Suddenly, the reporter who hailed from the Fujian province cursed in Yoyo's direction, loudly telling him to "shut the f*%# up". His outburst caused a stunned, momentary silence and a few stares in the newsroom. After realizing that the insensitive commentary hit a nerve and processing the scene that had just occurred, Yoyo tried to apologize. Anderson, their supervisor, walked briskly back to his office without saying anything further despite his role as a catalyst. Later that evening, as Yoyo was driving home with his nerves rattled, his phone rang. It quickly became apparent that Anderson's intention was to calm the waters, and near the end of the call he asked Yoyo to ignore the profane outburst in the interest of office harmony. He halfheartedly recognized his error, and sort of apologized for instigating the incident and the tension that ensued.

At that point Yoyo was continuing to apply for journalism work elsewhere, and he kept the faith that the police academy was still a real possibility going forward. Consequently, he was willing to put his job on the line in one brazen attempt to reduce the ongoing, unspoken toxicity in their newsroom. By early evening Yoyo had opened the bomb doors. He posted his frustrations in a lengthy message on the office WeChat, a group he knew included Anderson and a VP named Betty Lou. Without naming anyone in particular, he had hoped his sharply critical post would lead to one of two outcomes: *either Anderson would choose to reflect on his own behaviour and modify it, **and/or** some of his colleagues who were also feeling his harassment would step forward and validate his complaint.* In either case, Yoyo stated clearly that he just wanted to work in a far more enjoyable newsroom. Absent that, he was prepared to be reprimanded or fired for what would no doubt be perceived by some as a bold insubordination. Being bold at work is usually not the Chinese way.

In response to his online outburst, a Freemont VP contacted Yoyo the following week and asked him to file a formal complaint detailing his specific concerns. After a brief investigation, the Human Resources Department called him to a meeting where they handed him a letter of reprimand blaming him for engaging in offensive stereotypes and prejudicial commentary against ethnicities in China. He was asked to apologize again to the offended coworker. He saw that as reasonable and did so the next morning. He also promptly accelerated his online search for a new employer.

In the days and weeks that followed, the incident was never mentioned by anyone at work again, but Yoyo sometimes felt a chill while in the common areas with some of the other reporters. Oddly, Anderson stepped back and took a much more laissez-faire approach to managing Yo's work. Four weeks after he filed his complaint, and only three weeks after the meeting with HR, Anderson approached and asked Yo if he could stay late for a meeting after the others departed. He agreed and did some final edits on his report. When he entered the conference room and saw a woman he did not recognize, his heart got heavy. Yoyo quickly realized his time at Freemont was over, and he was very quiet as the HR representative explained the terms of severance and handed him his termination letter. With his mind racing as he was being terminated, Yo had trouble focusing on what they were saying. His memory of what his boss and the HR rep said was completely fragmented. It was much later that evening when Yoyo began to realize that something disingenuous and quite possibly unethical was happening. He and Kirk read the two page termination letter carefully, several times.

Freemont stated that the termination was <u>not</u> for cause; rather it was due to business challenges and "sustainability" issues deriving from the accelerating global Covid 19 pandemic. They said that he was the least tenured employee, so he was the one chosen for downsizing. Freemont told him he would receive one week's pay in lieu of notice, and they made his termination immediate. He was told that his benefits would be extended until July 10th, and wished him well with his future employment.

As they carefully reviewed the letter and the events of the past five weeks Kirk provided his support and counsel. The two of them peeled back the layers of the firing. They then reviewed the Employment Standards Act and relevant pages on the Labour Relations Board website. They were particularly focused on "just cause" and reprisal terminations. Within 24 hours it became fairly obvious to Yoyo that he could not, he would not, simply accept the terms. A fighter's instinct is to not stay down for long.

Consequently, on the second day of July, 2020, the Freemont Media President received a 'demand' letter (demand letters are the initial step recommended for the aggrieved when one's rights or laws are allegedly violated) written tersely - with a two week action deadline before Yoyo threatened to hire an employment lawyer. After two weeks of terse emails back and forth, Freemont caved late in the afternoon on the final day. In a stunning move, they offered Yoyo a new contract position in one of their other newsrooms, again in the role of Senior Writer/Reporter doing reports in Mandarin, with the same salary and an immediate reinstatement of all benefits. The badger found some honey in that beehive.

Chapter 22 *A Breakthrough*

Y oyo decided to back off from employment law litigation; he agreed to return to his job with Freemont, with the condition that he would be guaranteed no formal contact with his irritable former boss. During the next few months while in a much more enjoyable newsroom on a different floor of the building, Yo spent some time writing stories, and just as much time thinking about his next career move. He realized that Freemont was undervaluing him and underpaying not only him but all of their journalists, and he came to the conclusion that he was spinning his wheels working for a dead-end employer. He was considering all options, including leaving journalism entirely.

That summer Yoyo and Kirk and Mac took off for a few days to check out the rugged beauty of Ontario's Bruce Peninsula, and then they all spent the Labour Day weekend at an Airbnb on Lake Simcoe. It became clear to Yo that he had fallen in love with his new beau, so he did not look back. Fortunately, he and Tony had remained amicable despite the pain of their separation; they both began to accept their new situations. Tony even agreed to take care of Mac periodically, which was quite nice for everyone.

As 2020 gave way to a new year, Yoyo finished up his contract with Freemont. It was clear that although his second go-round with them would end more peacefully than his first, Freemont management would not keep him around in a new role. His final day would be February 1st. With so much change and stress occurring in such short order combined with differing desires regarding how to stay clear of the surging Covid virus, Yoyo and Kirk had some difficult days during the holiday season, their first Christmas together as a couple. Tony and his roommate Floyd were invited for a turkey dinner, which went well and everyone remained healthy for the holidays. Yoyo felt a mix of happiness and optimism as the year ended.

Meanwhile, Yoyo was monitoring LinkedIn and Indeed diligently in the first few weeks of 2021. He decided that if he could not land a job with a Canadian media business to do reporting in English, he would pivot away from journalism onto a different pathway. Throughout December and January Yoyo applied to virtually every single journalism related posting he found. He landed only one interview, with CTV news group. It did not go well. Ergo, Yoyo set his sights on his police college application – he was ready to park his 15 year career as a newsman behind him. After many weeks of soul searching and no income, Metroland Media Group *(Metroland is a division of the massive TorStar Corporation which owns and publishes over 70 regional and local papers / websites)* reached out regarding a reporter position writing for the Brampton Guardian. After that interview, but before he was even told if he was successful at securing that gig, one thing led to another and finally a breakthrough occurred: Yoyo was contacted by a different Metroland division to interview for a vacancy at the Richmond Hill Liberal and yorkregion.com. He was told that one of Metroland's best reporters was suddenly seconded to the parent company to write for the Toronto Star, creating an opportunity for Yoyo.

This, he decided, would be his last bullet. Although somewhat pessimistic at first, he spoke with Kirk about how to best prepare for the upcoming Zoom video conference interview. The two of them spent a few days mock interviewing using questions that his new partner prepared.

It was during one of those sessions that Yoyo found his footing and became more confident conversing about himself in interviews. Yoyo decided he would find a way to mention what he hoped would be his secret weapon - the new nickname Kirk lovingly labelled him with - *the Honey Badger.* A difficult panel interview occurred on a Monday morning, but by the end of the week Yoyo had reason to celebrate. Despite the offer being only a one year contract position without any benefits, Yoyo was ecstatic. He was being trusted with his first job writing in his second language, one of the official languages of his new country of residence. It had been almost 20 years since he had taught English in Tibet, and he was quite eager to prove his abilities to his new boss and to his colleagues.

Yo's new boss proved to be an absolute pleasure to work for. He was a performance focused mentor to Yoyo, and allowed his staff the right amount of autonomy. He was friendly and rarely called his staff so as to not interrupt workflow. He proved to be the kind of boss whose kindness one wants to reward. Despite no in-person contacts since all reporters worked in their home offices, the other beat writers scattered around York Region welcomed Yoyo warmly and provided tips and support during his challenging first month on the job. Kirk shared Yoyo's pride in his new position, in fact he provided some sources and editing support that Yoyo appreciated. His trio of reports about the impact of the pandemic on education was very well received, and was published less than eight weeks after he started working in that role. The stability of working at Metroland provided Yoyo with a sense of calm that he enjoyed as he wrote stories throughout 2021. In a nod to the nicknames the couple had created for one another, Yoyo wrote this bio which appears at the end of each of his reports:

Hold on Tight

Yoyo Yan has worked as a journalist since 2005 in various countries, including stints in China, Pakistan and Afghanistan. He is known to some as a honey badger for his curiosity and tenacity, which has allowed him to find and report on a wide array of stories in his career. He loves his American dingo (Mac) and his French bulldog (Kirk).

Late in the year Metroland management indicated that they were so pleased with his contributions that the York Region group would make room for him in a permanent role after his contract ended. All of that career development would be enough to lift anyone's spirits, but there was more, so much more to be stoked about during 2021…

Chapter 23 *Surrogacy Success*

D espite several years of disappointing results with the baby project, Yoyo remained determined to find the right woman to help him with his big goal. Yoyo had fronted nearly $15,000 to the FFC agency, but eventually gave up on them early in the year 2021. He and Kirk decided that would go in a different direction, so the two of them drafted a formal demand letter requesting a partial refund of the "matching" fees Yoyo had paid; although privately they thought that getting even one dollar back from a business after three years was a longshot. In a shocking development, management at FFC accepted their failure to deliver and promptly complied. They agreed to refund all but $1,800 of the fees they had taken. Yoyo was astounded that they were so amenable - and more to the point he was relieved to become so well-funded for the journey ahead.

Shortly thereafter, Yo decided to create a profile in his Facebook Group that he hoped would create some interest from a fertile and willing woman in Canada. Right after he decided to spend $25 to "boost" his surrogate wanted ad, several curious women responded. Yoyo had instant message chats with three of them before mulling over where to begin. A 10 minute FaceTime call with his first choice ensued. After the initial chat ended, Yoyo was bouncing off the walls with excitement; he really felt that an angel named Renee had descended from the heavens.

Renee seemed like a sincere person, and told the intended parents about herself. She explained that she already had three children and that she truly enjoyed being pregnant. Renee and her family were living a manageable distance (160 kilometers) from Toronto. She stated that since she had been blessed with children she often thought that one day she would like to play the role of surrogate for a couple of her choice, a couple who was eager to be parents but unable to conceive. Initially, the topic of compensation/money was not mentioned by either side; which, in hindsight, was another comforting fact for Yoyo. During their initial discussions Kirk was especially drawn to what they learned about Renee's career choice. She was a nurse; in fact she stated that she was a Victorian Order Nurse with a specialization in palliative (end-of-life) patient care. Renee's kindness, her sense of altruism, and her values seemed very apparent and sincere, so their first online meeting was a smashing success. Yoyo and Renee quickly agreed that they would like to meet again the following weekend.

Surrogate and intended parent matching is usually an extremely complex endeavour, and the counsellors at CReATe had advised Yoyo to take his time and ensure the woman chosen checked all the important boxes. Typically, in surrogacy situations it takes many months of phone calls, meetings, preparing legal documents and other events before an agreement to conceive can be completed. But Yoyo was feeling a sense of urgency as he approached his 40th birthday; not to mention his dismay with fielding all the questions from his parents, who could not understand why Yoyo and his "wife" were not parents yet.

In short order Yoyo reached out to his family lawyer friend who advised him of the contract creation process, required information he would have to gather, and her $3,000 legal fee. During his next few chats with Renee, Yoyo was able to gather the required data and made copious notes. After only three video calls it became very apparent to both Yoyo and Kirk that Renee was the real deal. She was extremely easy going and seemed willing to start the IVF process as soon as possible. Without ever having met in person, Yoyo took another leap of faith - he instructed the lawyer to draw up the formal surrogacy agreement so he could send it on to the agreeable angel.

Meanwhile, Yoyo contacted CReATe and informed them that he had a viable surrogate candidate who needed medical screening at their clinic. Renee signed the (expense reimbursement based) contract with only two minor edit requests, and on the first Wednesday in May the baby angel agreed to start the process. She needed to come into the Toronto clinic for her first appointment. Fortunately for her, Renee had the full support of her mother, who rode shotgun on the required commutes into the big city over the next few weeks. By early June Yoyo got the news he was yearning for. Renee was in good health and the clinic deemed her as an approved candidate for a frozen embryo transfer via IVF. She was placed on the required medications and told that the doctor could try to implant "embryo number 1" at 10 a.m. on the last day of June.

IVF procedures on women under the age of 35 have a fairly good chance of success, even more so when using a frozen embryo. During their earlier discussions Yoyo had asked Renee if she would agree to a second round of IVF if the first attempt failed. She agreed to include that request in the agreement without hesitation. Fortunately, a second attempt would not be necessary. Nearing the end of July Renee called Yoyo to tell him that her body felt different, and it was similar to how she felt early in her previous two pregnancies. A few days later, during her July 28th visit to the CReATe clinic, the doctor confirmed to Renee that a fetus was on board. Before getting in her car for the long ride home, Renee messaged Yoyo with the great news. He was euphoric, to the point of being almost speechless. It had been almost ten years of planning, setbacks, secrecy, and a separation....and now finally he felt the rush of success. If her pregnancy went well Yoyo and Kirk would welcome a spring baby, due March 25, 2022.

Meanwhile, Kirk and Yoyo were thinking about living space. Their current residence was a cozy three bedroom, one bath home with a renovated kitchen but no dining area. Yoyo often dreamed of having a large home where his family would visit often and there would be a playroom for the baby (or babies). Kirk, on the other hand, loved the modest bachelor pad and the gardens he had spent years improving, and was not in any hurry to relocate. The discussion about living space created somewhat of an impasse, including lengthy disagreements about the idea of knocking down exterior walls to add more space. But after some vigorous debate the couple reached a compromise; it would be status quo for at least one year after the birth of their baby - and they made an agreement to reassess their needs in 2023. Maybe if life was too chaotic and crowded in their Aurora residence, they would begin looking at larger homes. However, as we all know life is full of surprises...and they were totally unprepared for what happened next!

Only days after reaching their agreement to stay in Aurora and on a stellar summer evening, Kirk suggested they take Mac and go for a topless jaunt in the Jeep. Carrying the joyful news about their new pregnancy with them, they meandered happily around Newmarket taking in the sights and sounds of summer. Fatefully, Kirk eventually navigated the Jeep into old Newmarket to check out the unique white stucco, three-story facade of his grandparents' home; a beloved homestead his grandparents had owned for 53 years beginning in 1926. They later discovered that the 133 year old heritage residence had caring owners who financed many essential upgrades; the old gal was still looking stellar for her age. What was expected to be a tranquil evening joyride got a sudden surge of electricity when Kirk let out an animated shout after he noticed the large *for sale* sign on the front lawn.

Kirk's grandfather William narrowly missed a call to duty during World War I, which began just after his 21st birthday. Instead, he went to work as an accountant for the Canadian division of a successful, international, office equipment business founded in New York. He was a bachelor living near Newmarket, ON until he introduced himself to a lovely woman named Phyllis while killing time on the Yonge St streetcar. He and Phyllis Boulton Nordheimer, an heiress to a piano manufacturing business, fell in love and married in 1921. Four years later when they too were expecting their first child, they purchased a three story home in the heart of Newmarket, a small town north of Toronto that had been founded as a trading hub several decades earlier. The young couple did not move in right away, rather they chose to do a massive renovation project, adding rooms and altering the entire floor plan. In the end, they transformed their new home into a sprawling 3,500 square foot Edwardian style family home, complete with a housekeeper's suite on the upper floor.

Although his paternal grandmother, Phyllis, died the year before Kirk was born, Yoyo was aware that Kirk had a close relationship with his grandpa. There was a family gathering and formal dinner most Sundays from the time Kirk was in diapers until his grandfather's death when Kirk was 12. The layout of the old homestead had all sorts of amazing nooks and crannies, and featured a gardener's fantasy backyard almost the length of a soccer field. Kirk had fond memories of his time spent with his family and all the fun and games that ensued. For Kirk, the *for sale* sign immediately ignited a dormant desire to turn back time and take a tour of the old homestead.

Hold on Tight

Kirk and Yoyo arranged for a "showing" of the home the following day, and met the real estate agent at the front door; with absolutely no intentions other than satisfying their shared curiosity. The Newmarket resident/agent, Keith Ward, who appeared to be in his 70s, welcomed them and explained that this home had a special appeal to him, since he had admired it on his walks to school as a boy. He seemed quite pleased to be hired as the listing agent, and told Kirk a quick story about meeting his grandfather. He said that after approaching the massive old oak front door and summoning the courage to ring the bell one summer day; and the realtor told them that he was invited in for tea and snacks by the much older patriarch. Upon hearing that, Kirk was stunned by the coincidence so many years later, and quite intrigued.

After touring the property and being advised of the dozens of home improvements the sellers had completed over their 20 years of ownership, Kirk and Yoyo excused themselves and had a private chat in the living area. Kirk had come to the realization that maybe this was more than a one-time tour; and wanted his partner's initial reaction to the idea of pursuing a deal for the heritage home. Although Yoyo had some reservations they decided to ask about how motivated the sellers were, and what their floor sale price might be at that point. They were told that the home had been on the market for almost three months, and the sellers were "running out of runway" because they needed to move it and many of their furnishings so they could embark on a much anticipated 10 month trip on their yacht. A motivated seller was music to their ears, so the band played on.

After two days of discussions and financing calculations, Kirk and Yoyo became more and more excited about the idea of raising their baby in such a classic old home. Kirk decided to simply hire the vendor's agent so that the agent would be super motivated to get it done, and then made an offer just below list price. The sellers, who had put so much time and effort into their residence, were surprised to learn that there was such rich family history included in the source of their first fair offer. A deal with the two soon-to-be mariners was quickly consummated, and on the last day of September, about six months before their due date, Kirk and Yoyo relocated to a classic three-story home in Newmarket.

Owning an aging home proved to be almost a full time job in itself for Kirk and Yoyo. Over the first few months, the couple worked at a furious pace to upgrade the antiquated and inefficient heating system, design a completely new master bathroom, create a well-equipped nursery, and improve the two decks. They wanted to have the house in good order prior to their little bundle's arrival in the springtime. The whole operation became a labour of love.

Meanwhile, the IVF pregnancy was normal in every way, without complications. Renee lived a healthy lifestyle and saw her doctor regularly. With unbridled anticipation, a formal announcement to friends and family was made on Thanksgiving Day. The excited parents could just not wait any longer to share their wonderful news. Declarations of surprise and warm wishes followed from near and far, and by Christmas the nursery was full of gifts. As the calendar turned to 2022, they had only 11 more weeks to prepare for Lillian's arrival...and still one diabolical dilemma to deal with.

Chapter 24 *The Revelation*

A lthough homosexuality is no longer illegal in China, the searing *social stigma* remains. In Yoyo's parents' generation the concept of a same-sex couple committing to one other and raising a family is unfathomable. In fact, most Chinese families take the "Don't Ask Don't Tell" approach to the topic of sexuality. Yoyo confided to Kirk that he actually sensed his parents know he is queer, and they were likely very distressed about it. They did not want to discuss it and most certainly did not want it known to others. Regardless, Yoyo felt a strong urge to share his real life with his parents…..but how? He was extremely conflicted since he did not want them to feel shocked or ashamed. And he certainly did not want them to perceive him as mentally ill or 'deficient' in any way. He needed them to realize that he was, is, and will always be the same good son. One day he hoped they would understand that human attraction and sexuality is uncontrollable - and more importantly he dreamed of a day that they would accept that "love is love".

With the baby entering the third trimester in early January, Yoyo felt strongly that this was the time to venture out of the closet and come clean with his parents about his sexuality and his same-sex relationships; what he termed his "real life". He remained hopeful that his mother would be willing and able to travel to Canada and share the joy of taking care of a baby together. Meiying, his only sister, had been trusted with her brother's big secret for many years. Yo knew she too would have concerns about rocking their parents' world with this raucous revelation, but he was increasingly certain that Meiying would support his coming out plan.

Somewhere around that time Yoyo became inspired by American gay footballer Colton Underwood's coming-out story, which was delivered via a popular Netflix documentary. He became convinced that creating a short secret sharing documentary would be the best way to unleash himself from his heavy emotional chains. With the help of a videographer friend Yoyo directed and starred in a six minute video, made exclusively for his parents. They would finally learn the truth about his two marriages and his life with Tony and then Kirk; with a little bit of surrogacy education embedded into the revelations.

While all that was going on Yoyo began to converse with his sister back in Beijing. After years of hesitancy, Meiying agreed that it was probably the right time. One day while having a shopping day with her mom, Meiying found a way to test the waters regarding the imminent bombshell.

Meiying said: (translated from Mandarin)

"Mom, you know that Zhonghua no longer lives with Ada, right?"

Mother: "Yes, how sad your father and I are."

Meiying: "I know. She was a nice girl but the truth is that marriage was never going to work out. Do you know why their relationship ended, Mom?"

Mother: "Not really. I have asked Zhonghua only twice about Ada and he gave me no good information."

Meiying:	"Well Mom, life is not as simple as it once was. The truth is that Zhonghua is now certain that he prefers the company of men. That is why he left the marriage with Ada...to pursue a different kind of relationship."
Mother:	"A different kind? Meiying what on Earth do you mean?"
Meiying:	"What I mean is...(pauses to find the right words) Zhonghua is living with a man in Canada, and he tells me that he is in love with this man. This is sometimes called a same-sex couple or same-sex relationship. In fact, millions of younger Chinese men and women are doing the same."
Mother:	"No, it cannot be true Meiying. That's not real."
Meiying:	"Mom, in the next few days, Zhonghua plans to tell you and dad this secret, and he really wants you to accept his life and not be upset about all of this."

Four days later, on a Friday night when he knew his parents would be almost ready to awaken in Beijing, Yoyo uploaded his startling documentary to WeChat, took a deep breath, and finally hit *send*. Very shortly thereafter and before he even hit his pillow, Yoyo received a three emoji thumbs-up WeChat reply from dad. Instantly, he felt lighter.

His mother, a woman of tradition and closed mind, reacted differently. She chose to be silent for a few days. Eventually, mom agreed to video chat with Yoyo and although she did not tell him she still loved him and accepted his life, Yoyo felt a conversation was a start on her journey to acceptance. After the call Yoyo told Kirk that his mother thought the whole situation was only a phase, without permanency. He was hoping all she would need was some time.

Suddenly it was January, and time for Yoyo and his mother to make a big decision....would grandma still want to use her existing visa to travel to Canada to support Yoyo and be another caregiver, given that she would have to be fully immersed in his non-traditional family? Despite her disdain, she agreed to go. Evidently, the lure of being with the new baby was powerful regardless of the living arrangements, so Yoyo promptly arranged and paid for her flight.

Chapter 25 *Lovely Little Lillian*

G randma-to-be Yan arrived at Pearson International Airport the day after Valentine's Day, about four weeks prior to Renee's due date. Kirk played the role of chauffeur and waited curbside while Yoyo excitedly jumped out of the car to meet his mother at arrivals. Once they arrived in Newmarket, grandma settled into her second floor guest room and spent a few days overcoming jet lag after her 25 hour, connection-filled, trek to the other side of the world. Shortly thereafter she was busy organizing the nursery to her liking and preparing spicy Szechuan meals for Yoyo on a daily basis.

Meanwhile, in a stroke of supremely good fortune, Yoyo's contract at Metroland Media ended on March 11th. Although he was very much enjoying working for Metroland, the expiration of his contract allowed Yoyo and Kirk two full weeks of final preparations before the little bundle rocked their world.

The daddies-to-be had a decision to make, but actually they had no problem deciding on a name for their little munchkin. She would be named Lillian. That name holds a very special appeal for Kirk since his mother Teresa's sister was named Lillian, or Lil as she was known to her loved ones. Teresa and Lil were very close, they lived together for quite a long time in Montreal before Teresa met the love of her life, Mike. Kirk's Aunt Lillian and her husband Leo ended up having four beautiful children, the youngest of whom is named Colleen.

Colleen and Kirk lived in different provinces but the two cousins still became quite close in their formative years. Sadly, when Colleen was quite young Lillian's life was cut short with inoperable cancer. She was only 44 years of age. It was a devastating loss for the entire family, and his mother Teresa's grieving was seared into her son's memory.

Yoyo wholeheartedly agreed that Lillian was the best name to choose for their little munchkin. His parent's surnames are Li and Yan, both of which are nicely embedded. They also both agreed that the two common abbreviations people will use for Lillian (Lily and Lil) are lovely as well.

Their nursery had all the essentials at that point - it just needed a baby! That problem would be solved soon enough. On a Thursday one week prior to the due date, Yoyo received the message he was waiting for from Belleville. In a surprising turn of events, Renee said that her doctor felt it was optimal to induce labour after 39 weeks of pregnancy for IVF babies. Ergo, they decided that she would be given an injection the next day at 17:00. Labour would begin within hours. Renee told Yoyo that she really hoped that the daddies-to-be would be able to make the trip on short notice, since she had chosen Yoyo as her "birthing partner" – meaning he would be the only non-medical person allowed in the delivery room.

By 15:00 the next day the expecting parents had the "baby bag" packed and the car was heading east for a two hour ride to Belleville. Upon arrival at the hospital Kirk waited while Yoyo raced up to join Renee on the 6th floor maternity ward. Shortly after midnight the labour pains began and the birth partners stayed up all night talking and waiting. Just before sunrise the doctor on duty was summoned and Renee was moved swiftly into the delivery room. Then, at 07:59, on the third Saturday in March, 2022, Lillian took her first breath….a breath that took Yoyo's away.

Chapter 26 *Princess Joy*

L ater that day the two new daddies came to a sudden realization – it is hard to believe that we will all be heading home so soon! They discovered that the helpless infant training session lasts for only 24 hours, when the nurses provide their wisdom and guidance. But within hours after a birth they start talking about an imminent departure from their ward. 'What? Are you telling us that we have to leave the friendly confines of the hospital tomorrow, and we are on our own? You know that we haven't done this before, right?' The word panic may not have been the correct descriptor here, but it is certainly close!

Nonetheless, on Sunday morning the new parents carefully strapped little Lil into her car seat, thanked the nurses, and headed for home. With a mixture of joy and anxiety, Kirk steered the car onto the highway and began driving more cautiously than at any time since his licensing road test some 40 years prior. They arrived home safely in the early afternoon Sunday and were greeted by one excited new grandmother, and by a happy, if slightly confused, dog.

The parents decided that Lillian's full name should be registered as **Lillian McCaffrey Yan**, with the understanding that when Lil turns 18, she could choose to reverse the secondary names to have either the Irish surname or leave it as is, selecting the Chinese surname as her legal name. While obviously a bit unusual, the objective was to give Lillian as much control as possible in her life. Additionally, Yoyo provided their little girl with a Chinese nickname which translates to English as "Princess Joy".

Lillian was examined by two nurses and two doctors in the first week of her life, with no concerns. She acclimated smoothly to napping in her 100 year old family heirloom bassinet, took the bottle every three hours, and for the first few weeks little Lil barely cried at all. Remarkably, she was sleeping soundly through the night at ten weeks. Her much anticipated first smile came at seven weeks, and by June Lillian was responding to stories her daddy told her with heartwarming cooing and shrieks of delight. Yoyo's devoted mother stayed in Canada for months to take good care of her third grandchild, giving the new daddies' ample time to rest.

Lillian continued to be showered with gifts and frequent visits from family members like Barb, Mel & Raegan, Uncle John, Aunt Vicki and cousin Emma, Heather and Sean, Paula and Gerald, the wonderful Hay family and Auntie Meiying; and her adoring Godmothers Jaclyn and Colleen. She also received visits and special gifts throughout spring and summer from close friends Tony (Godfather), Floyd, and Dianne Stevens; the Lusk and the Moore families; and lots of new neighbours like Davy and Shauna, Pat and Anne, Diane and Beric, Elaine and Fred, the incredibly generous Jelena and Matt (the adoring parents of toddlers Olive and Ruby), and even Newmarket Mayor John Taylor.

It quickly became evident to Kirk and Yoyo that they had been blessed with an abundance of clothing, books, a stellar new baby carriage – and also with lots of love, kindness, and good parental advice. All they really needed to do was **Hold Her Tight.**

Manufactured by Amazon.ca
Bolton, ON

27234779R00097